Taste *of* Home

KIDS CAN COOK!

THIS BOOK BELONGS TO:

_____

_____

DATE: _____

©2025 RDA Enthusiast Brands, LLC.
1610 N. 2nd St., Suite 102, Milwaukee WI
53212-3906

Visit us at **tasteofhome.com** for other
Taste of Home books and products.

International Standard Book Number:
979-8-88977-104-3

Chief Content Officer: Jason Buhrmester
Content Director: Mark Hagen
Creative Director: Raeann Thompson
Associate Creative Director:
Jami Geittmann
Senior Editor: Christine Rukavena
Senior Art Director: Courtney Lovetere
Assistant Art Director: Carrie Peterson
Manager, Production Design:
Satyandra Raghav
Assistant Art Director (Production):
Jogesh Antony
Print Publication Designer:
Nithya Venkatakrishnan
Deputy Editor, Copy Desk: Ann M. Walter
Senior Copy Editor: Suchismita Ukil
Copy Editor: Rayan Naqash

Cover Food Photography:
Taste of Home Photo Studio

Pictured on front cover: Heart's Desire
Pizza, p. 202; Orange Party Punch, p. 135;
Watermelon Rice Krispies Treats, p. 214;
Princess Toast, p. 15; Puppy Dog Cake,
p. 236; Marshmallow Fruit Dip, p. 151

Pictured on back cover:
Disney's Dole Whip, p. 138;
Taco Salad Waffles, p. 19

Cover Photography:
Andersen Ross Photography Inc/Getty
Images (back cover, upper left corner)

Interior Photography:
Getty Images: Cavan Images, p. 9;
Kmatta, p. 23; kali9, p. 49

Photos via Submission: Images of
kids cooking submitted by TMB staff &
loved ones

All other images copyright Trusted Media
Brands, Inc.

Printed in China
1 3 5 7 9 10 8 6 4 2

CONTENTS

KIDS REALLY CAN COOK!

BUILD SKILLS. FEED YOUR FAMILY. HAVE FUN!

Your kitchen adventure starts here! It's time to cook up the snacks you crave,
make delicious meals for your family, and have fun along the way!

HOW TO USE THIS BOOK

Find a Recipe for Your Skill Level.

Our Skill Level Guide makes it easy to find recipes for your age and cooking abilities.
Just remember that every kid is different. Check in with a grown-up before you get started.

Great for most kids—easy
assembly and no handling of
hot foods. (Always have help
chopping food, and working
the oven and other appliances.)

Suitable for older kids:
There may be some chopping,
boiling water, browning foods
on the stovetop and handling
of hot foods.

For skilled cooks—may require
good hand-eye coordination
or timing. Family members
might make these recipes as
a team.

Choose a Dish That Catches Your Eye.

Every recipe has a photo, so you know what you'll get! Just flip through a chapter that interests you.

Watch Out for These Icons.

The **Mixing Bowl** marks recipes that are perfect for any kid to make—no chopping,
no heat and little danger. Beginners can make many of these all by themselves!

The **Stop Sign** indicates recipes that must be made with an adult's supervision.
Techniques like deep-frying, broiling, campfire cooking and grilling can be dangerous.
Never try these recipes without an adult's help, even if you're a big kid.

Check for Ingredients and Equipment.

Before you jump in, peek at the lists that start each recipe—they'll tell you what you need.

Missing something? That's often not a problem! Swapping or skipping ingredients or tools can be part of the adventure. In fact, that's how new, tasty recipes are made! If you're unsure, ask an experienced cook to help you come up with fun alternatives.

Stay Safe!

Cooking uses lots of skills—some that involve sharp tools and hot surfaces. That's why safety comes first! Always ask an adult for permission to cook, and talk through your plan with them. As you gain experience cooking with this book, your family will learn what you can safely do on your own and when you should have a helping hand.

Here Are Some Ideas to Get Started.

Below, we've broken down some common kitchen tasks by age. Talk with an adult about where you fit!

AGES 3-5	AGES 5-7	AGES 8-12	AGES 13 & UP
Wash fruits and vegetables	Mix dry ingredients	Peel veggies	Make recipes on the stovetop
Tear lettuce for salads	Measure and count items	Toast bread & make sandwiches	Bake on your own
Mash ingredients	Roll cookie dough or meat into balls	Simple heating in microwave	Learn to use other appliances
Wrap potatoes in foil to bake	Set the table	Wash and put away dishes	Clean up
Smash graham crackers for crusts	Chop softer fruits and veggies	Pack your own lunch	Use sharp knives
Knead dough	Crack eggs	Unload groceries	Plan meals
Scoop batter for muffins & cupcakes	Read the recipe steps aloud	Mix batters and doughs	Try new recipes, make dinner

Food Safety Basics

To make sure your food is free from harmful germs, follow these simple but important rules.

START OUT CLEAN.
Wash your hands, cutting boards and utensils with hot, soapy water before and after handling uncooked food. Make sure everything you need is clean and dry before you begin.

KEEP FOODS SEPARATE.
Don't let raw meat touch foods that won't receive any further cooking. In the refrigerator, store raw meats on lower shelves (below other foods), and use a pan, bag or plate to catch drips. Always wash tools and hands after handling meat. And no need to rinse raw meat—it will only spreads germs in the sink.

WATCH THE TEMPERATURE.
Keep hot foods at 140° or warmer, and cold foods at 40° or cooler. Use slow cookers, a warming drawer or ice to help. Don't leave food out at room temperature for more than 2 hours (or 1 hour on hot days).

GETTING STARTED

Basic Equipment You'll Need

COOKWARE

▲ Dutch oven

Skillet with lid ▶

Skillet ▶

▲ Saucepan

Pan with ▶ wire rack

BAKEWARE

◀ Muffin tin

◀ Round cake pans

15x10x1-in. baking pan ▼

◀ Baking pans or dishes

Square ▶ baking pan

Loaf pan ▲

How to Set the Table

For a basic place setting, put the dinner plate in the center. The fork goes to the left of the plate, while the knife is on the right with its blade facing in. Place spoon beside the knife. Add a glass above the knife. The napkin can either go under the fork or on top of the plate.

OTHER EQUIPMENT

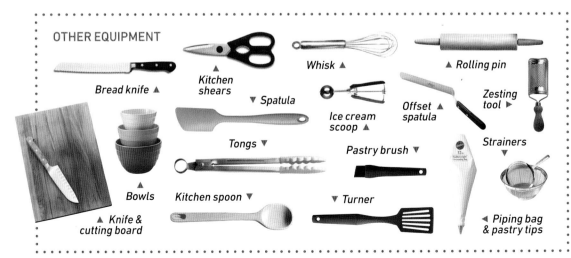

Bread knife ▲

Kitchen shears ▲

Whisk ▲

▲ Rolling pin

▼ Spatula

Ice cream scoop ▲

Offset ▲ spatula

Zesting tool ▶

Tongs ▼

Pastry brush ▼

Strainers ▼

Bowls ▲

Kitchen spoon ▼

▼ Turner

▲ Knife & cutting board

◀ Piping bag & pastry tips

How to Measure Ingredients

1. LIQUIDS
Place your measuring cup on a flat surface and check at eye level. For sticky stuff like honey, spray the cup with cooking spray first—it makes cleanup easier!

4. OTHER INGREDIENTS
Spoon ingredient into the cup until it overflows. Then level off the top with a flat edge, removing any extra.

2. FLOUR
Fluff up the flour with a spoon, and then scoop it into a dry measuring cup. Let it overflow and use a flat edge to scrape off the extra.

5. SMALL AMOUNTS WITH MEASURING SPOONS
Fill the spoon with dry ingredients, like spices or baking powder, then level it off. For liquids, hold the spoon over a small bowl to catch any spills.

3. BROWN SUGAR
Pack brown sugar tightly into the measuring cup with your fingers or a spoon. It should hold its shape when tipped out!

6. BUTTER, CREAM CHEESE & STICK SHORTENING
Check the markings on the wrapper to find the right amount, then slice with a knife. If ingredients don't come in a wrapper, measure as for other ingredients in no. 4 at left.

Kitchen Math Is Easy Math

3 teaspoons (tsp.)	=	1 tablespoon (Tbsp.)
16 tablespoons (Tbsp.)	=	1 cup
2 cups	=	1 pint
2 pints	=	1 quart (qt.)
4 quarts (qt.)	=	1 gallon
16 ounces (oz.)	=	1 pound (lb.)
1 ounce (oz.)	=	28 grams (g)

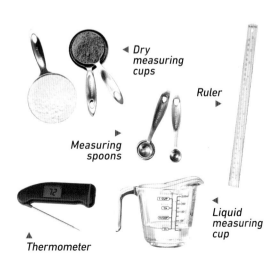

◄ Dry measuring cups

Ruler ►

Measuring spoons ►

◄ Liquid measuring cup

▲ Thermometer

PAGE
20

YUMMY TUMMY

(IDEAS FOR PARTICULARLY LITTLE COOKS)

SKILL LEVEL 1

Chicken Nugget Casserole

Our kids love to eat chicken nuggets this way. It's a satisfying supper with spaghetti and a salad on the side.

—Tylene Loar, Mesa, AZ

INGREDIENTS

- 1 pkg. (13½ oz.) frozen chicken nuggets
- ⅓ cup grated Parmesan cheese
- 1 jar (24 oz.) pasta sauce
- 1 cup shredded part-skim mozzarella cheese
- 1 tsp. Italian seasoning

EQUIPMENT

- 11x7-in. baking dish
- Spatula
- Measuring cups

PREP: 5 min. • **BAKE:** 30 min. • **MAKES:** 6 servings

1. Preheat oven to 350°. Place chicken nuggets in a greased 11x7-in. baking dish. Sprinkle with Parmesan cheese. Using a spatula, spread with pasta sauce. Top with the mozzarella cheese and Italian seasoning.

2. Cover and bake until chicken is heated through and cheese is melted, 30-35 minutes.

1 SERVING 306 cal., 17g fat (5g sat. fat), 36mg chol., 968mg sod., 23g carb. (10g sugars, 4g fiber), 15g pro.

> **"Tastes fancy and uses stuff we love."**
> —SOPHIA K., AGE 5

You'll need half an 8-oz. bag of shredded cheese.

"You can never have
too many sprinkles."

—ROBIN C., AGE 3

SKILL LEVEL 2

Birthday Cake Freezer Pops

On my quest to find birthday cake ice cream—my favorite flavor— I came up with these easy ice pops. Now, instead of going to the store whenever a craving hits, I just head to my freezer.
—**Dawn Lopez, Westerly, RI**

PREP: 25 min. + freezing • **MAKES:** 1½ dozen

INGREDIENTS

- ⅔ cup sprinkles, divided
- 18 disposable plastic or paper cups (3 oz. each)
- 2 cups cold 2% milk
- 1 pkg. (3.4 oz.) instant vanilla pudding mix
- 1 carton (8 oz.) frozen whipped topping, thawed
- 2 cups crushed vanilla wafers (about 60 wafers)
- 18 wooden pop sticks

EQUIPMENT

- Measuring cups & spoons
- Pop molds & sticks
- Large bowl
- Whisk
- Kitchen spoon
- Piping bag

1. Spoon 1 tsp. sprinkles into each cup.

2. In a large bowl, whisk milk and pudding mix for 2 minutes. Let stand until soft-set, about 2 minutes. Stir in the whipped topping, crushed wafers and remaining sprinkles.

3. Cut a 1-in. hole in the tip of a piping bag or in a corner of a food-safe plastic bag; fill bag with pudding mixture. Pipe into prepared cups. Top cups with foil and insert pop sticks through foil.

4. Freeze until firm, about 4 hours. Let stand at room temperature 5 minutes before gently removing pops.

1 POP 161 cal., 7g fat (3g sat. fat), 4mg chol., 96mg sod., 23g carb. (15g sugars, 0 fiber), 1g pro. **DIABETIC EXCHANGES** 1½ starch, 1½ fat.

Fancy Ice Cream Sandwiches

Place a decoration (such as **Teddy Grahams**, crushed **pretzels** or **cookies**, **sprinkles** or **M&Ms**) in a shallow bowl. Let the **ice cream sandwich** soften a bit, then press the ice cream into the decoration. Refreeze your fancy sandwiches if needed.

INGREDIENTS

- 1 cup confectioners' sugar
- 2 Tbsp. milk
- ⅛ tsp. almond extract
- 1 medium apple, sliced
- 1 tsp. creamy peanut butter
- 2 fresh thyme sprigs, optional
- 1 small pear, sliced
- 1 clementine, peeled
- 2 fresh strawberries, cut in half lengthwise
- 1 small cluster green grapes
- ¼ cup unsalted cashews

EQUIPMENT

- Small bowl
- Whisk
- Cutting board & knife
- Measuring cups & spoons

Hungry Fruit Caterpillar

Party snacks can be good for you! Arrange fresh fruit in the shape of a caterpillar. Get creative and use what foods you like best. Be sure an adult does all the cutting.

—Kim Mordecai, Little Rock, AR

PREP: 20 min. • **MAKES:** 4 servings

1. In a small bowl, whisk confectioners' sugar, milk and extract until smooth; set aside.

2. Cut apple lengthwise in half; place 1 half on a serving platter. Cut remaining half into slices. Cut eyes from 1 slice.

3. Using peanut butter, attach apple pieces for eyes and a cashew half for a mouth. If desired, attach thyme sprigs for antennae. Arrange apple slices and remaining fruit in a wavy pattern to form the caterpillar body. Place the cashews under caterpillar for legs; serve with glaze.

1 SERVING 250 cal., 1g fat (0 sat. fat), 1mg chol., 83mg sod., 61g carb. (41g sugars, 3g fiber), 2g pro.

Rainbow Berries

Melt **candy coating disks** in a microwave, then add **food coloring** to make your favorite shade. Dip **strawberries** in coating, decorate if you'd like, then let dry on parchment or waxed paper. Use orange coating to make cute carrots for Easter!

SKILL LEVEL **1**

INGREDIENTS

6 slices white bread, toasted

6 Tbsp. seedless strawberry jam

1½ cups buttercream frosting (in assorted colors)

6 Tbsp. sprinkles

6 tsp. silver or gold edible glitter

EQUIPMENT

- Toaster
- Butter knives or small offset spatulas
- Bowls

Princess Toast

I made these sparkly treats for my daughter's Brownie troop. They're great for princess parties too. Sometimes I use lemon curd instead of jam.

—Marina Castle Kelley, Canyon Country, CA

TAKES: 10 min. • **MAKES:** 6 servings

Spread jam over toast. Top with buttercream, sprinkles and edible glitter. Leave toasts whole or cut into shapes.

NOTE Edible glitter is available from Wilton Industries; visit wilton.com.

1 PIECE 465 cal., 13g fat (5g sat. fat), 0 chol., 284mg sod., 82g carb. (58g sugars, 1g fiber), 3g pro.

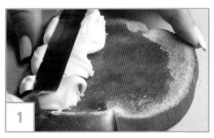

How to Decorate Princess Toast

STEP 1: To make striped toast, put a blob of each color frosting on a piece of toast.

STEP 2: Then smear frosting across the toast with an offset spatula.

WANT SWIRLED TOAST? Add blobs of different colors, then swirl and spread the frosting with a butter knife. Let the combinations create their own colors—where pink and blue frostings mix, for example, you'll get a purple color.

SKILL LEVEL 1

INGREDIENTS

- 1 **can (20 oz.) crushed pineapple, undrained**
- 1 **can (21 oz.) cherry or blueberry pie filling**
- 1 **pkg. yellow cake mix (regular size)**
- ¾ **cup butter, melted**

EQUIPMENT

- **13x9-in. baking dish**
- **Spatula**
- **Liquid measuring cup**

Pineapple Cherry Cake

When our granddaughter visits on weekends, I try to find something fun for her to do. Since packaged ingredients are simply layered in a pan, this is an easy treat that even a young child can fix.
—Melissa Defauw, Auburn Hills, MI

PREP: 5 min. • **BAKE:** 50 min. • **MAKES:** 16 servings

1. Preheat oven to 350°. Evenly sprinkle pineapple in a greased 13x9-in. baking dish. Using a spatula, gently spread with the pie filling. Sprinkle with the dry cake mix. Place the butter in a liquid measuring cup; drizzle butter over the top. Give the pan a small shake to work the butter down into the cake mix.

2. Bake until top is golden brown, 50-60 minutes.

1 SERVING 275 cal., 12g fat (6g sat. fat), 23mg chol., 297mg sod., 42g carb. (28g sugars, 1g fiber), 2g pro.

★★★★★

"I have also used strawberry pie filling. We call this a dump cake. It's so quick and simple, my 7-year-old makes it. Excellent served warm with vanilla ice cream. Yummy!"
—FAITH1109, TASTEOFHOME.COM

"Taco waffles, please!"
—ABIGAIL P., AGE 5

SKILL LEVEL 2

Taco Salad Waffles

Taco salad is a popular Mexican fare standby, but this recipe turns it into a build-your-own main dish. I've also served it as a brunch option.

—Trisha Kruse, Eagle, ID

TAKES: 25 min. • **MAKES:** 4 servings

INGREDIENTS

- 1 **lb. ground beef**
- 1 **cup salsa**
- 1 **can (4 oz.) chopped green chiles**
- 1 **envelope taco seasoning**
- 8 **frozen waffles**

   Optional: Shredded cheddar cheese, shredded lettuce, chopped tomatoes, cubed avocado, salsa and sour cream

EQUIPMENT

- **Large skillet**
- **Kitchen spoon**
- **Measuring cup**
- **Baking sheet or toaster**
- **Bowls**

1. In a large skillet, cook beef over medium heat until no longer pink; drain. Stir in the salsa, chiles and taco seasoning. Bring to a boil. Reduce heat; simmer for 5 minutes.

2. Meanwhile, toast the waffles according to package directions, using a baking sheet or toaster. Serve waffles with beef mixture and toppings of your choice.

2 WAFFLES 460 cal., 20g fat (6g sat. fat), 80mg chol., 1664mg sod., 43g carb. (5g sugars, 2g fiber), 25g pro.

DIY Dinners

Taco bars are fun because everybody gets to make their dinner just how they want, using their own favorite toppings. Pizza bars, sandwich bars with different meats, cheeses and veggies, and baked potato bars are terrific ideas too.

Abigail P. likes melted cheese, tomatoes, guacamole and salsa on her taco waffles.

INGREDIENTS

1 **cup peanut butter**

1 **cup sugar**

1 **large egg, room temperature**

1 **tsp. vanilla extract**

30 **milk chocolate kisses**

EQUIPMENT

- **Measuring cup & spoon**
- **Mixer or kitchen spoon**
- **Baking sheets**
- **Wire racks**

Peanut Butter Kiss Cookies

Everyone who tries these delicious gems is amazed that they use only five ingredients. Baking cookies doesn't get much easier than this.
—**Dee Davis, Sun City, AZ**

PREP: 20 min. • **BAKE:** 10 min./batch • **MAKES:** 2½ dozen

1. Preheat oven to 350°. Cream peanut butter and sugar until light and fluffy, 5-7 minutes. Beat in egg and vanilla.

2. Roll into 1¼-in. balls. Place 2 in. apart on ungreased baking sheets. Bake until tops are slightly cracked, 10-12 minutes. Immediately press 1 chocolate kiss into center of each cookie. Cool for 5 minutes before removing from pans to wire racks.

1 COOKIE 102 cal., 6g fat (2g sat. fat), 7mg chol., 43mg sod., 11g carb. (10g sugars, 1g fiber), 2g pro.

★★★★★

"Absolutely great. I'm only 12 years old, and I make them all by myself."

—**JSALDIERNA, TASTEOFHOME.COM**

SKILL LEVEL 1

INGREDIENTS

- 3 Tbsp. chocolate syrup, divided
- 3 scoops chocolate or vanilla ice cream
- 1 cup chilled club soda

  Optional toppings: Sliced banana, honey-roasted peanuts, cut-up peanut butter cups, animal crackers, whipped cream and maraschino cherries

EQUIPMENT

- Measuring cup & spoon
- Ice cream scoop

Jungle Float

This fun floats lets kids (and adults, too) be the masters of their own creations. What a tasty way to experiment!
—Jenni Sharp, Milwaukee, WI

TAKES: 5 min. • **MAKES:** 1 serving

Place 2 Tbsp. chocolate syrup in a tall glass. Add the ice cream and remaining chocolate syrup. Top with club soda. Garnish with toppings of your choice. Serve immediately.

1 SERVING 578 cal., 22g fat (13g sat. fat), 67mg chol., 238mg sod., 92g carb. (83g sugars, 2g fiber), 9g pro.

Strawberry Cream Float

Place 2 Tbsp. **strawberry jam** in a tall glass; stir in 1 tsp. **water** to thin it slightly. Top with 2 scoops **strawberry ice cream**, 3 sliced **strawberries**, ¼ cup **cream** and **strawberry soda** or **sparkling water**. Top with whipped cream and sprinkles if desired.

PAGE 46

GOOD MORNING, SUNSHINE!

Ham & Swiss Omelet

Whether you make this easy omelet for breakfast or dinner, it's sure to get rave reviews.

—Agnes Ward, Stratford, ON

INGREDIENTS

- 1 Tbsp. butter
- 3 large eggs
- 3 Tbsp. water
- ⅛ tsp. salt
- ⅛ tsp. pepper
- ½ cup cubed fully cooked ham
- ¼ cup shredded Swiss cheese

EQUIPMENT

- **Small nonstick skillet**
- **Measuring cups & spoons**
- **Bowl**
- **Whisk**
- **Spatula**

TAKES: 20 min. • **MAKES:** 1 serving

1. In a small nonstick skillet, melt butter over medium-high heat. Whisk the eggs, water, salt and pepper. Add egg mixture to skillet (mixture should set immediately at edges).

2. As eggs set, push cooked edges toward the center, letting uncooked portion flow underneath. When the eggs are set, place ham on 1 side and sprinkle with cheese; fold the other side over filling. Slide omelet onto a plate.

1 OMELET 510 cal., 37g fat (18g sat. fat), 655mg chol., 1495mg sod., 2g carb. (1g sugars, 0 fiber), 41g pro.

  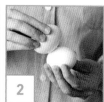 

How to Crack an Egg (2 Ways)

#1 ON THE COUNTER
- Gently but firmly rap the center of the egg against the countertop.
- Use your thumbs to press inward and separate the shell, then pour the yolk and white into a bowl.

#2 WITH TWO EGGS
- Hold an egg in each hand. Tap the eggs together at their centers. One egg will crack.
- Use your thumbs to press inward and separate the shell.

"Cooking breakfast with the boys is a great way to start the day! They slide a chair over to the counter, hop on up, and start cracking eggs."
—ADAN F., DAD

SKILL LEVEL 3

INGREDIENTS

- 1 pkg. (¼ oz.) active dry yeast
- 1 tsp. sugar
- ½ cup warm water (110° to 115°)
- 2 cups warm 2% milk (110° to 115°)
- 2 large eggs, room temperature
- ½ cup butter, melted
- 2¼ cups all-purpose flour
- 1 tsp. salt
- ⅛ tsp. baking soda

EQUIPMENT

- Bowls
- Measuring cups and spoons
- Kitchen spoon
- Waffle maker

Light-as-Air Waffles

These terrific waffles are crispy on the outside and tender on the inside. Never too filling, they leave room for sampling the rest of the brunch buffet.

—Helen Knapp, North Pole, AK

PREP: 15 min. + rising • **BAKE:** 5 min./batch • **MAKES:** 10 waffles

1. Dissolve yeast and sugar in warm water; let stand 5 minutes. Beat in milk, eggs and butter.

2. In another bowl, combine flour, salt and baking soda; stir into yeast mixture just until combined. Cover and let rise in a warm place until doubled, about 45 minutes.

3. Stir batter. Bake in a preheated waffle maker according to the manufacturer's directions until golden brown.

2 WAFFLES 453 cal., 23g fat (14g sat. fat), 131mg chol., 726mg sod., 49g carb. (6g sugars, 2g fiber), 12g pro.

Spiced Yeast Waffles Add ¼ tsp. vanilla extract to the milk and stir in ¼ tsp. each ground nutmeg or cinnamon along with the flour.

How to Keep Waffles Hot

If you're feeding a crowd, place the cooked waffles in a single layer on a baking sheet in a 200° oven. You can keep them hot for about half an hour. After that, they'll start to dry out.

SKILL LEVEL **1**

INGREDIENTS

- 1 lb. reduced-fat bulk pork sausage
- 2 cups all-purpose flour
- ¼ cup sugar
- 1 Tbsp. baking powder
- 1 tsp. salt
- ½ tsp. ground cinnamon
- ¼ tsp. ground nutmeg
- 1 large egg, room temperature, lightly beaten
- 2 cups fat-free milk
- 2 Tbsp. canola oil
- 2 Tbsp. honey

   Maple syrup, optional

EQUIPMENT

- Mini muffin tins
- Ruler
- Baking pan with rack
- Bowls
- Measuring cups & spoons
- Whisk
- Kitchen spoon
- Wire racks

Pigs in a Pool

My kids love sausage and pancakes, but making them for breakfast on a busy weekday was out of the question. My homemade version of pigs in a blanket is a thrifty alternative to the packaged kind, and they freeze like a dream.
—**Lisa Dodd, Greenville, SC**

PREP: 45 min. • **BAKE:** 20 min. • **MAKES:** 4 dozen

1. Preheat the oven to 350°. Coat 48 mini muffin cups with cooking spray.

2. Shape sausage into forty-eight ¾-in. balls. Place meatballs on a rack coated with cooking spray in a shallow baking pan. Bake until cooked through, 15-20 minutes. Drain on paper towels.

3. In a large bowl, whisk flour, sugar, baking powder, salt and spices. In another bowl, whisk egg, milk, oil and honey until blended. Add to flour mixture; stir just until moistened.

4. Place a sausage ball in each mini muffin cup; cover with batter. Bake until lightly browned, 20-25 minutes. Cool 5 minutes before removing from pans to wire racks. Serve warm, with syrup if desired.

FREEZE OPTION Freeze cooled muffins in airtight freezer containers. To use, microwave each muffin on high until heated through, 20-30 seconds.

4 MINI MUFFINS 234 cal., 10g fat (3g sat. fat), 45mg chol., 560mg sod., 26g carb. (9g sugars, 1g fiber), 10g pro. **DIABETIC EXCHANGES** 1½ starch, 1 medium-fat meat, ½ fat.

"This is my kids' favorite breakfast treat! Make a batch or two and freeze them. Five stars!"
—**AMANDALINA03, TASTEOFHOME.COM**

SKILL LEVEL 2

INGREDIENTS

- 6 slices day-old Texas toast
- 4 large eggs
- 1 cup 2% milk
- 2 Tbsp. sugar
- 1 tsp. vanilla extract
- ¼ to ½ tsp. ground cinnamon
- 2 cups crushed cornflakes, optional
- Confectioners' sugar, optional
- Maple syrup

EQUIPMENT

- Knife & cutting board
- 13x9-in. dish
- Large bowl
- Measuring cups & spoons
- Whisk
- 15x10x1-in. pan
- Freezer container

French Toast Sticks

Keep these French toast sticks in the freezer for an instant breakfast. Their handy size makes them ideal for munching on the go.
—*Taste of Home* Test Kitchen

PREP: 20 min. + freezing • **BAKE:** 20 min. • **MAKES:** 1½ dozen

1. Cut each slice of bread into thirds; place in a single layer in an ungreased 13x9-in. dish. In a large bowl, whisk eggs, milk, sugar, vanilla and cinnamon. Pour over bread; soak for 2 minutes, turning once. If desired, coat bread with cornflake crumbs on all sides.

2. Place in a greased 15x10x1-in. pan. Freeze until firm, about 45 minutes. Transfer to an airtight freezer container and store in the freezer.

TO USE FROZEN FRENCH TOAST STICKS Place desired number on a greased baking sheet. Bake at 425° for 8 minutes. Turn; bake 10-12 minutes longer or until French toast sticks are golden brown. Sprinkle sticks with confectioners' sugar if desired. Serve with syrup.

3 STICKS 183 cal., 6g fat (2g sat. fat), 145mg chol., 251mg sod., 24g carb. (8g sugars, 1g fiber), 8g pro.

The Game Plan

LITTLE KIDS CAN ...
Gather food and equipment, whisk the egg mixture and dip the French toast sticks in cornflakes.

BIG KIDS CAN ...
Cut bread into sticks, pour the egg mixture, freeze and bake the French toast sticks.

INGREDIENTS

1½ cups 2% milk

2 cups frozen cubed pineapple

1 medium banana, peeled, quartered and frozen

Honey, optional

EQUIPMENT

• Blender

• Measuring cup

Frozen Tropical Smoothies

This pineapple and banana smoothie with take you to the tropics. Try the frosty drink with a squeeze of lime juice.
—*Taste of Home* Test Kitchen

TAKES: 10 min. • **MAKES:** 2 servings

Place the first 3 ingredients in a blender; cover and process until blended. If desired, add honey to taste.

2 CUPS 227 cal., 4g fat (2g sat. fat), 15mg chol., 88mg sod., 44g carb. (32g sugars, 4g fiber), 8g pro.

It's Science!

Frozen ingredients make a thicker smoothie than cold or room-temperature ones. If you don't already have a frozen banana, you don't have to wait to make this smoothie. You can use a plain banana instead and add some ice cubes or other frozen foods like berries, mango or even spinach to make the smoothie thick and frosty.

SKILL LEVEL 2

INGREDIENTS

- 2 slices sourdough bread
- 1 Tbsp. mayonnaise
- 1 large egg
- 1 slice cheddar cheese
- 2 cooked bacon strips

EQUIPMENT

- Biscuit cutter
- Measuring spoon
- Butter knife
- Large skillet with lid
- Turner

Toad in the Hole Bacon Sandwich

Switch up the cheese—pepper jack gives a nice kick—or use sliced kielbasa, ham or sausage in place of the bacon in this versatile grilled cheese sandwich.

—Kallee Krong-McCreery, Escondido, CA

TAKES: 15 min. • **MAKES:** 1 serving

1. Using a biscuit cutter or round cookie cutter, cut out center from 1 slice of bread (discard center or save for another use). Spread mayonnaise on 1 side of both bread slices. In a large skillet coated with cooking spray, lightly toast slice with cutout, mayonnaise side down, over medium-low heat. Flip slice; crack an egg into center. Add remaining bread slice, mayonnaise side down, to skillet; layer with cheese and bacon.

2. Cook, covered, until egg white is set, yolk is soft-set and cheese begins to melt. If needed, flip bread slice with egg to finish cooking. To assemble sandwich, use solid slice as bottom and cutout slice as top.

1 SANDWICH 610 cal., 34g fat (11g sat. fat), 240mg chol., 1220mg sod., 46g carb. (4g sugars, 2g fiber), 30g pro.

How to Bake Bacon

Place a wire rack in a baking pan. Line up bacon strips on the rack and bake at 350° until crisp, 15-20 minutes. Carefully remove the pan from the oven or let the bacon cool with the oven off and door ajar. (Grease in the pan will be hot.)

French Toast Waffles

I'm a from-scratch cook but also like shortcuts. Since we love French toast and waffles, I use a waffle maker to make a hybrid French toast.

—Linda Martindale, Elkhorn, WI

PREP: 15 min. • **COOK:** 5 min./batch • **MAKES:** 16 waffles

INGREDIENTS

- 8 large eggs
- 2 cups 2% milk
- ½ cup sugar
- 1 tsp. vanilla extract
- ½ tsp. ground cinnamon
- ½ tsp. ground nutmeg
- 16 slices Texas toast
- Maple syrup

EQUIPMENT

- Large bowl
- Measuring cups & spoons
- Whisk
- Waffle maker
- Tongs

In a large bowl, whisk the first 6 ingredients until blended. Dip both sides of bread in egg mixture. Place in a preheated waffle maker; bake until golden brown, 4-5 minutes. Serve with syrup.

FREEZE OPTION Cool waffles on wire racks. Freeze between layers of waxed paper in freezer containers. Reheat frozen waffles in a toaster on medium setting.

2 WAFFLES 340 cal., 9g fat (3g sat. fat), 192mg chol., 476mg sod., 51g carb. (19g sugars, 2g fiber), 14g pro.

Waffles with Whimsy

Use sliced cinnamon-raisin bread or brioche in this recipe. Instead of—or in addition to—maple syrup, serve the waffles with whipped cream in a can and fresh berries.

Sophia P., age 1, loves marshmallows, whipped cream, and chocolate and caramel sauces on her waffles. Her sister Abigail, age 5, prefers chocolate chips and whipped cream.

SKILL LEVEL 2

Freezer Breakfast Sandwiches

On a busy morning, these freezer breakfast sandwiches save the day. A hearty combo of eggs, Canadian bacon and cheese will keep you fueled until lunchtime.

—Christine Rukavena, Milwaukee, WI

PREP: 25 min. • **BAKE:** 15 min. • **MAKES:** 12 sandwiches.

INGREDIENTS

12 large eggs

⅔ cup 2% milk

½ teaspoon salt

¼ teaspoon pepper

SANDWICHES

12 English muffins, split

4 tablespoons butter, softened

12 slices Colby-Monterey Jack cheese

12 slices Canadian bacon

EQUIPMENT

- Large bowl
- Measuring cups & spoons
- Whisk
- 13x9-in. baking pan
- Wire rack
- Toaster or baking sheet
- Butter knife
- Knife
- Offset spatula

1. Preheat oven to 325°. In a large bowl, whisk eggs, milk, salt and pepper until blended. Pour into a 13x9-in. baking pan coated with cooking spray. Bake until set, 15-18 minutes. Cool on a wire rack.

2. Meanwhile, toast English muffins (or bake at 325° until lightly browned, 12-15 minutes). Spread 1 tsp. butter on each muffin bottom.

3. Cut eggs into 12 portions. Using an offset spatula, layer each muffin bottom with an egg portion, a cheese slice (tearing the cheese to fit) and a Canadian bacon slice. Replace muffin tops. Wrap sandwiches in waxed paper and then in foil; freeze in a freezer container.

TO USE FROZEN SANDWICHES Remove foil. Microwave a waxed paper-wrapped sandwich at 50% power until thawed, 1-2 minutes. Turn sandwich over; microwave at 100% power until hot and a thermometer reads at least 160°, 30-60 seconds. Let stand 2 minutes before serving.

1 SANDWICH 334 cal., 17g fat (9g sat. fat), 219mg chol., 759mg sod., 26g carb. (3g sugars, 2g fiber), 19g pro.

How to Rise & Shine

Customize these sandwiches with different types of cheese, fully cooked sausage patties or bacon strips instead of Canadian bacon, or by using only eggs. Label the sandwiches so family members can find their favorites.

INGREDIENTS

- ¾ cup peanut butter
- 12 slices bread
- 6 Tbsp. jelly or jam
- 3 large eggs
- ¾ cup 2% milk
- ¼ tsp. salt
- 2 Tbsp. butter

EQUIPMENT

- Butter knives
- Large bowl
- Measuring cup and spoons
- Whisk
- Large skillet
- Turner

PB & J French Toast

I've always tried to make cooking fun for myself, my daughters and my grandkids. Cooking teaches children the importance of following directions and organization. This recipe is easy to make, and kids really like it.
—Flo Burtnett, Gage, OK

TAKES: 20 min. • **MAKES:** 6 servings

1. Spread peanut butter on 6 slices bread; spread jelly on the remaining 6 slices. Put 1 slice of each together to form a sandwich; repeat. In a large bowl, whisk the eggs, milk and salt. Dip both sides of sandwiches in egg mixture.

2. In a large skillet, melt butter over medium heat. Cook the sandwiches for 2-3 minutes on each side or until golden brown.

1 SANDWICH 450 cal., 22g fat (5g sat. fat), 96mg chol., 567mg sod., 50g carb. (20g sugars, 3g fiber), 16g pro.

"This was so good! Made for my mother and she flipped over it. She now has this at least once a week."
—AMEHART, TASTEOFHOME.COM

SKILL LEVEL 1

INGREDIENTS

- 1 cup cherry juice blend
- ¾ cup vanilla yogurt
- 1 medium ripe banana, cut into chunks
- 1 cup frozen unsweetened blueberries
- ½ cup crushed ice

  Dash ground cinnamon

EQUIPMENT

- Blender
- Measuring cups
- Knife & cutting board

Blueberry & Banana Smoothies

Our ripest bananas go straight into the blender for this favorite beverage. The flavor combo is fabulous for breakfast on the go or as a snack between meals.
—**Lisa DeMarsh, Mount Solon, VA**

TAKES: 5 min. • **MAKES:** 3 servings

In a blender, combine all ingredients; cover and process for 30 seconds or until smooth. Pour into glasses; serve immediately.

1 CUP 164 cal., 2g fat (1g sat. fat), 6mg chol., 44mg sod., 33g carb. (26g sugars, 2g fiber), 4g pro.

How to Blend Smoothies

Always place liquid in the blender first. Liquid over the blades helps get the mixing going. Top the liquids with solids, like fruit, veggies and ice. Hold the lid on securely while running the blender.

"The kitchen can get messy, but I need to try to stay clean."

—LANCE S., AGE 3

Fluffy Scrambled Eggs

When our son, Chris, wants something other than cold cereal in the morning, he whips up these eggs. Cheese and evaporated milk make them especially good. They're easy to make when you're camping too.

—**Chris Pfleghaar, Elk River, MN**

TAKES: 15 min. • **MAKES:** 3 servings

In a bowl, whisk eggs, milk, salt and pepper. In a large skillet, heat oil over medium heat. Pour in egg mixture. Add cheese dip; stir into eggs with a spatula or kitchen spoon. Cook and stir eggs until thickened and no liquid egg remains.

½ CUP 246 cal., 18g fat (6g sat. fat), 438mg chol., 523mg sod., 4g carb. (4g sugars, 0 fiber), 15g pro.

INGREDIENTS

- 6 large eggs
- ¼ cup evaporated milk or half-and-half cream
- ¼ tsp. salt
- ⅛ tsp. pepper
- 1 Tbsp. canola oil
- 2 Tbsp. cheese dip

EQUIPMENT

- Bowl
- Measuring cup and spoons
- Whisk
- Large skillet
- Spatula or kitchen spoon

Make It Your Own!

There are lots of ways to get creative with your morning scramble. Here are some ideas to get you started.

PICK PRODUCE. Add your favorite veggie mix-ins, such as sauteed peppers, onions, mushrooms or spinach.

ADD MEAT. Turn your eggs into a heartier skillet meal by adding in chopped-up ham or cooked breakfast sausage.

EXPERIMENT WITH HERBS. Have fresh herbs on hand? Add them to your eggs! Basil, dill and chives all are great stirred into fluffy scrambled eggs. You can also raid the spice rack. Add a few dashes of garlic powder, paprika or cayenne.

MAKE A FACE. Arrange toppings like olives, tomatoes, green onions and cheese on your plated eggs to create fun faces.

WRAP IT UP. Fill soft tortillas with scrambled eggs. Add cheese, salsa and your favorite taco toppings.

SKILL LEVEL 2

Light & Fluffy Pancakes

I found this fluffy pancake recipe among our old family favorites and adapted it to make a small amount. It's quick and easy to prepare, but we still consider it a special treat.

—Eugene Presley, Council, VA

TAKES: 15 min. • **MAKES:** 8 pancakes

INGREDIENTS

- 1 cup all-purpose flour
- 1 Tbsp. sugar
- 2 tsp. baking powder
- ½ tsp. salt
- 1 large egg, room temperature
- ¾ cup 2% milk
- ¼ cup shortening or butter, melted

EQUIPMENT

- Bowls
- Measuring cups & spoons
- Whisk or kitchen spoon
- Griddle or large skillet
- Turner

1. In a small bowl, combine flour, sugar, baking powder and salt. Combine egg, milk and shortening; stir into dry ingredients just until moistened.

2. Pour batter by ¼ cupfuls onto a greased hot griddle. Turn when bubbles form on top of pancakes; cook until the second side is golden brown.

2 PANCAKES 269 cal., 14g fat (8g sat. fat), 81mg chol., 666mg sod., 29g carb. (5g sugars, 1g fiber), 6g pro.

Hop, Hop, Hooray!

Use a squeeze bottle to make pancakes in fun shapes, like ovals for bunny feet and triangles for bunny ears. Make a tail with a dollop of whipped cream and fuzz it up with shredded coconut.

"My big brother and my mom taught me how to make these! It's fun to try new toppings."

-PAIGE W., AGE 11

How to Flip Pancakes

STEP 1: Wait until bubbles form on the pancake and the edge begins to set. Gently slide a turner under the pancake.

STEP 2: Lift and flip the pancake in a smooth motion. If the pancake splats a bit, just use the turner to push any loose batter back into the pancake. Wait longer to flip your next pancake.

SKILL LEVEL **2**

INGREDIENTS

2½ cups frozen shredded hash brown potatoes

⅓ cup chopped onion

3 Tbsp. butter

5 large eggs

½ cup 2% milk

1 tsp. Italian seasoning

½ tsp. salt

½ tsp. pepper

25 slices pepperoni

1 cup shredded Mexican cheese blend

EQUIPMENT

- **Large skillet with lid**
- **Measuring cups & spoons**
- **Knife & cutting board**
- **Kitchen spoon**
- **Large bowl**
- **Whisk**

Pepperoni Hopple-Popple

My grandma and I created this kid-friendly version of a German breakfast dish. Serve it with toast or English muffins.

—Jaycee Gfeller, Russell, KS

TAKES: 30 min. • **MAKES:** 6 servings

1. In a large skillet, cook potatoes and onion in butter until tender and lightly browned. Meanwhile, in a large bowl, whisk eggs, milk, Italian seasoning, salt and pepper.

2. Pour over egg mixture over potato mixture. Sprinkle with the pepperoni. Cover and cook on medium-low heat until eggs are set, 10-12 minutes. Remove from the heat. Sprinkle with cheese; cover and let stand for 2 minutes. Cut into 6 wedges.

1 PIECE 267 cal., 20g fat (11g sat. fat), 219mg chol., 608mg sod., 9g carb. (2g sugars, 1g fiber), 12g pro.

The Game Plan

LITTLE KIDS CAN ...
Gather food and equipment, crack eggs, whisk the egg mixture and count the pepperoni.

BIG KIDS CAN ...
Chop the onion, set a kitchen timer and work the stovetop.

SKILL LEVEL 3

INGREDIENTS

- 1 unsliced loaf (1 lb.) French bread
- 4 Tbsp. butter, softened, divided
- 2 Tbsp. mayonnaise
- 8 thin slices deli ham
- 1 large tomato, sliced
- 1 small onion, thinly sliced
- 8 large eggs, lightly beaten
- 8 slices cheddar cheese

EQUIPMENT

- Bread knife & cutting board
- Knife
- Butter knives
- Measuring spoon
- Whisk
- Large skillet
- Kitchen spoon

Ham & Egg Sandwich

Whenever the whole family gets together for a holiday or long weekend, they request this big breakfast sandwich. I can feed everyone by stacking our favorite breakfast fixings inside a loaf of French bread. Then I simply pop it in the oven to warm up.

—DeeDee Newton, Toronto, ON

PREP: 30 min. • **BAKE:** 15 min. • **MAKES:** 8 servings

1. Preheat oven to 375°. Cut bread in half lengthwise; carefully hollow out top and bottom, leaving ½-in. shells (discard removed bread or save for another use). Spread 3 Tbsp. butter and all of the mayonnaise inside bread shells. Line bottom bread shell with ham; top with tomato and onion.

2. In a large skillet, melt remaining butter; add eggs. Cook over medium heat, stirring occasionally until edges are almost set.

3. Spoon into bottom bread shell; top with cheese. Cover with bread top. Wrap in greased foil. Bake 15-20 minutes or until heated through. Cut into serving-size pieces.

1 SERVING 543 cal., 31g fat (14g sat. fat), 298mg chol., 1644mg sod., 33g carb. (3g sugars, 2g fiber), 32g pro.

> **"These taste good because we made them with teamwork!"**
> **—DELANEY W., AGE 5**

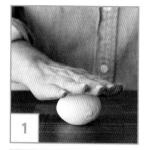

How to Peel Hard-Boiled Eggs

STEP 1: Roll the hard-boiled egg back and forth on a hard surface until the shell is completely cracked.

STEP 2: Start peeling from the large end of the egg—it will help separate the thin membrane underneath the shell from the egg's surface. If needed, swish the egg around in a bowl of cold water to remove any bits of remaining shell.

SKILL LEVEL 3

Breakfast Pigs in a Blanket

Hard-boiled eggs and sausages wrapped up crescent dough make for the breakfast version of the classic pig in a blanket. They're perfect for those days when you want to stay curled up in your blanket.

—James Schend, Pleasant Prairie, WI

TAKES: 30 min. • **MAKES:** 2 dozen

INGREDIENTS

- 4 **hard-boiled large eggs**
- 1 **tube (8 oz. refrigerated crescent rolls**
- 12 **cooked breakfast sausage links, cut in half widthwise**
- 12 **cherry tomatoes, halved**
- 1 **large egg**
- 1 **Tbsp. poppy seeds**

EQUIPMENT

- **Knife & cutting board**
- **Baking sheet**
- **Fork**
- **Pastry brush**

1. Preheat oven to 325°. Cut each egg into 6 wedges.

2. Unroll crescent dough and separate into 8 triangles; cut each triangle lengthwise into 3 thin triangles.

3. Place 1 sausage piece on the wide end of each smaller triangle; top with an egg wedge and a cherry tomato half. Roll up tightly; place point-side down on a parchment-lined baking sheet.

4. Beat egg with a fork. Brush beaten egg over pastries; sprinkle with poppy seeds. Bake until golden brown on bottom and heated through, 14-16 minutes.

1 PIECE 83 cal., 5g fat (1g sat. fat), 45mg chol., 195mg sod., 5g carb. (1g sugars, 0 fiber), 4g pro.

Hard-Boiled Eggs

Place **eggs** in a single layer in a large saucepan; add enough **cold water** to cover by 1 in. Cover and quickly bring to a boil. Remove pan from the heat. Let stand for 15 minutes for large eggs (18 minutes for extra-large eggs and 12 minutes for medium eggs). Rinse eggs in cold water, then place in ice water to cool. Drain and refrigerate.

SKILL LEVEL 3

Birthday Pancakes

I try to make special foods for my kids, especially on their birthdays. To transform plain old pancake mix, I add cake mix and sprinkles. Frosting closes the deal.

—Dina Crowell, Fredericksburg, VA

PREP: 15 min. + standing • **COOK:** 5 min./batch • **MAKES:** 6 servings

INGREDIENTS

- 1 cup pancake mix
- 1 cup yellow or white cake mix
- 2 large eggs, room temperature
- 1½ cups plus 1 Tbsp. 2% milk, divided
- 1 tsp. vanilla extract
- ¼ cup sprinkles
- ¾ cup vanilla frosting
  Additional sprinkles

EQUIPMENT

- Bowls
- Measuring cups & spoons
- Whisk
- Kitchen spoon
- Griddle or large skillet
- Turner
- Microwave
- Spatula

1. Whisk pancake mix and cake mix. In a separate bowl, whisk the eggs, 1½ cups milk and vanilla until blended. Add to dry ingredients, stirring just until moistened. Let stand 10 minutes. Fold in ¼ cup sprinkles.

2. On a lightly greased griddle over medium heat, pour batter by ¼ cupfuls to create 6 large pancakes. Cook until bubbles on top begin to pop; turn. Cook until golden brown. Repeat, using smaller amounts of batter to create pancakes of different sizes.

3. Microwave frosting and remaining milk, covered, on high until melted, 10-15 seconds. Stir with a spatula until smooth. On each of the large pancakes, layer smaller pancakes in order of decreasing size with the smallest on top; drizzle with frosting. Top with additional sprinkles.

1 SERVING 396 cal., 12g fat (3g sat. fat), 67mg chol., 558mg sod., 65g carb. (38g sugars, 1g fiber), 7g pro.

Celebration Stack

Any time is a good time for a towering stack of pretty flapjacks. Try heart sprinkles and pink icing for Valentine's Day or confectioners' sugar and snowflake sprinkles at Christmas. Or celebrate the big game with your team's colors.

Stella R.'s favorite part of making these is flipping the pancakes. It's like a game to see if she can catch them in the pan without dropping them!

"Do you think the
pancake is as
big as my face?"
—STELLA R., AGE 7

PAGE
78

LUNCH
ON THE GO

SKILL LEVEL 1

Country Ham Sandwiches

This yummy sandwich is perfect for lunches or a quick weeknight dinner when there's no time for a big meal. Smoked cheddar and a creamy garlic-infused spread lend special appeal to this easy handheld.

—Jennifer Parham, Browns Summit, NC

TAKES: 5 min. • **MAKES:** 2 servings

In a small bowl, combine the mayonnaise, sour cream and garlic powder with a spoon. Using a butter knife, spread mixture over 2 slices of bread. Layer each with a slice of cheese, tomato, ham and lettuce. Top with remaining bread.

1 SANDWICH 538 cal., 30g fat (11g sat. fat), 75mg chol., 1323mg sod., 41g carb. (13g sugars, 8g fiber), 28g pro.

INGREDIENTS

- 2 **Tbsp. mayonnaise**
- 2 **Tbsp. sour cream**
- ⅛ **tsp. garlic powder**
- 4 **slices whole wheat bread**
- 2 **oz. smoked cheddar cheese, sliced**
- 4 **slices tomato**
- 4 **oz. thinly sliced deli ham**
- 2 **lettuce leaves**

EQUIPMENT

- **Small bowl**
- **Measuring spoons**
- **Spoon**
- **Butter knife**
- **Knife & cutting board**

Join the Club

This take on the classic club sandwich is inspired by fancy hasselback potatoes. With a serrated knife, slice a plum tomato partway through. Then tuck your favorite sandwich fixin's inside.

Want some creative ways to keep lunch cold? Freeze pudding snack cups, fruit cups or yogurt pouches and use them as ice packs. Or wash and freeze seedless grapes and pack them in a food bag.

How to Make Bread Crumbs

Tear soft white bread into pieces and place in a food processor or blender. Cover and pulse until crumbs form. Your appliance may have a pulse button. Push it on and off quickly, or push the power button the same way to pulse ingredients. Pulsing helps you chop a food without turning it into paste. You'll need 1 or 2 slices of bread to make 1 cup of crumbs.

If you don't have a food processor or blender, tear 2 slices of bread into tiny pieces with your hands. Your meatballs will have a more rustic texture, which is OK!

INGREDIENTS

- 1 cup soft bread crumbs
- ¾ cup 2% milk
- 2 large eggs, lightly beaten
- ½ cup grated Parmesan cheese
- ¾ tsp. salt
- ½ tsp. garlic powder
- ½ tsp. pepper
- 2 lbs. bulk mild Italian sausage

SOUP

- 4 cups beef stock
- 1 jar (24 oz.) marinara sauce
- 3 cups water
- 1 tsp. dried basil
- 8 oz. angel hair pasta, broken into 1½-in. pieces

  Additional grated Parmesan cheese, optional

EQUIPMENT

- Large bowl
- Measuring cups & spoons
- Kitchen spoon
- 15x10x1-in. baking pan with rack
- 6-qt. slow cooker

Slow-Cooker Spaghetti & Meatball Soup

A couple of nights a week our family is going every which way, all at the same time. A hearty soup is an easy way to give us all a warm meal. Angel hair is thinner than spaghetti, so it cooks quickly.
—Susan Stetzel, Gainesville, NY

PREP: 45 min. • **COOK:** 6¼ hours • **MAKES:** 8 servings (3 qt.)

1. Preheat oven to 400°. In a large bowl, mix bread crumbs and milk. Let stand 5 minutes; drain. Stir in the eggs, cheese and seasonings. Add sausage; mix lightly but thoroughly. Shape into 1-in. balls. Place meatballs on a greased rack in a 15x10x1-in. baking pan. Bake until cooked through, 12-15 minutes.

2. Transfer meatballs to a 6-qt. slow cooker. Add stock, marinara sauce, water and basil. Cook, covered, on low 6-8 hours to allow flavors to blend.

3. Stir in the pasta; cook, covered, on high until pasta is tender, 15-20 minutes longer. If desired, serve with additional cheese.

1½ CUPS 394 cal., 26g fat (9g sat. fat), 95mg chol., 1452mg sod., 23g carb. (9g sugars, 2g fiber), 17g pro.

"The entire family loves this. I use frozen meatballs when I'm in a hurry."
—CARRIE CARNEY, TASTEOFHOME.COM

SKILL LEVEL **2**

Classic Macaroni Salad

This recipe is a refreshingly light take on an all-time favorite. It's perfect for a fast weeknight dinner or a festive weekend barbecue.

—Dorothy Bayes, Sardis, OH

TAKES: 30 min. • **MAKES:** 8 servings

1. Cook macaroni according to package directions; drain and rinse with cold water. Cool completely.

2. For dressing, in a small bowl, combine the mayonnaise, pickle relish, sugar, mustard, salt and pepper. In a large bowl, combine the macaroni, celery, carrot and onion. Add dressing and toss gently to coat.

3. Refrigerate until serving. Garnish with egg and paprika.

¾ CUP 115 cal., 2g fat (0 sat. fat), 27mg chol., 362mg sod., 21g carb. (6g sugars, 2g fiber), 4g pro. **DIABETIC EXCHANGES** 1½ starch.

> ## "One of my favorite lunches!"
> **—ELLIE K., AGE 7**

INGREDIENTS

- 2 **cups uncooked elbow macaroni**
- 1 **cup fat-free mayonnaise**
- 2 **Tbsp. sweet pickle relish**
- 2 **tsp. sugar**
- ¾ **tsp. ground mustard**
- ¼ **tsp. salt**
- ⅛ **tsp. pepper**
- ½ **cup chopped celery**
- ⅓ **cup chopped carrot**
- ¼ **cup chopped onion**
- 1 **hard-boiled large egg, chopped**
- **Dash paprika**

EQUIPMENT

- Pot & strainer for macaroni
- Measuring cups & spoons
- Kitchen spoons
- Bowls
- Knife & cutting board

How to Chop Eggs with a Cooling Rack

No egg chopper? No problem! Set a grid-style rack on top of a bowl and smoosh the peeled egg through.

SKILL LEVEL 3

INGREDIENTS

- 1 Tbsp. butter
- 2 celery ribs, sliced
- ½ cup chopped onion
- 3 cups frozen mixed vegetables (about 15 oz.)
- 1 can (10¾ oz.) condensed cream of chicken soup, undiluted
- ½ cup 2% milk
- ½ tsp. onion powder
- ¼ tsp. garlic salt
- ⅛ tsp. dried thyme
- ⅛ tsp. pepper
- 2 cups cubed cooked chicken breast
- 2 tubes (12 oz. each) small refrigerated flaky biscuits (10 count)

EQUIPMENT

- Large skillet
- Knife & cutting board
- Measuring cups & spoons
- Kitchen spoon
- Rolling pin
- Ruler
- Muffin tins

Chicken Little Pies

I made these personalized chicken potpies in muffin tins for my kids, and they gobbled them up. For the record, the grown-ups did too!

—Melissa Haines, Valparaiso, IN

PREP: 30 min. • **BAKE:** 15 min. **MAKES:** 10 servings

1. Preheat oven to 375°. In a large skillet, heat butter over medium heat; saute celery and onion until tender, 4-5 minutes. Stir in vegetables, soup, milk and seasonings; heat through, stirring occasionally. Stir in chicken; remove from heat.

2. On a lightly floured surface, roll each biscuit into a 5-in. circle. Press each onto the bottom and up side of each of 20 greased muffin cups, allowing edges to extend above cups. Fill each with about 3 Tbsp. chicken mixture. Pull up edges of dough and fold partway over filling, pleating as needed.

3. Bake until crusts are golden brown and filling is bubbly, 15-18 minutes. Cool 1 minute before serving.

2 MINI POTPIES 330 cal., 12g fat (4g sat. fat), 28mg chol., 1049mg sod., 39g carb. (7g sugars, 3g fiber), 15g pro.

★ ★ ★ ★ ★

"I made these for my grandson. So yummy and tasty. The only change I made was using chicken gravy mix in place of the soup and milk, as we have a dairy sensitivity. Would make again. Everyone enjoyed them."

—GUEST2378, TASTEOFHOME.COM

SKILL LEVEL **2**

INGREDIENTS

- 1 **medium onion, chopped**
- 1 **small green pepper, chopped**
- 1 **small sweet yellow pepper, chopped**
- 1 **Tbsp. canola oil**
- 1 **garlic clove, minced**
- 1 **lb. ground turkey**
- 1 **can (15 oz.) solid-pack pumpkin**
- 1 **can (14½ oz.) diced tomatoes, undrained**
- 4½ **tsp. chili powder**
- ¼ **tsp. salt**
- ¼ **tsp. pepper**

  Optional toppings: Shredded cheddar cheese, sour cream, corn chips and sliced green onions

EQUIPMENT

- **Large skillet**
- **Knife & cutting board**
- **Measuring spoons**
- **Kitchen spoon**
- **3-qt. slow cooker**

Slow-Cooker Pumpkin Chili

We have this chili often because everyone loves it—even the most picky grandchildren. It's a definite keeper in my book!

—Kimberly Nagy, Port Hadlock, WA

PREP: 20 min. • **COOK:** 7 hours • **MAKES:** 4 servings

1. In a large skillet, saute onion and peppers in oil until tender. Add garlic; cook 1 minute longer. Crumble turkey into skillet. Cook over medium heat until meat is no longer pink.

2. Transfer to a 3-qt. slow cooker. Stir in the pumpkin, tomatoes, chili powder, salt and pepper. Cover and cook on low for 7-9 hours. Serve with toppings as desired.

1¼ CUPS 281 cal., 13g fat (3g sat. fat), 75mg chol., 468mg sod., 20g carb. (9g sugars, 7g fiber), 25g pro. **DIABETIC EXCHANGES** 3 lean meat, 1 starch, 1 vegetable, 1 fat.

Did You Know?

Green peppers are unripened versions of red, yellow or orange peppers. They are cheaper than colored peppers because farmers can pick them right away instead of waiting for them to ripen.

Colored peppers add more sweetness to a dish. Green peppers actually taste a little "green"—as in, not ripe.

It's good to use lots of natural colors in your diet. It boosts the range of healthy chemicals you're getting from your veggies. This chili has veggies in five different colors!

SKILL LEVEL 1

Pigs in a Blanket

These baked hot dog sandwiches appeal to kids of all ages. Even my husband, Allan, admits to enjoying every bite! We like to dip them in ketchup and mustard.

—**Linda Young, Longmont, CO**

TAKES: 25 min. • **MAKES:** 4 servings

1. Preheat oven to 375°. Separate crescent dough into triangles. Place hot dogs at wide ends of triangles and roll up. Place on an ungreased baking sheet. With a fork, combine egg and water; brush over rolls. Sprinkle caraway seeds over tops; press lightly into the rolls.

2. Bake 12-15 minutes or until golden brown.

2 SANDWICHES 516 cal., 39g fat (12g sat. fat), 97mg chol., 1365mg sod., 27g carb. (8g sugars, 0 fiber), 16g pro.

INGREDIENTS

- 1 tube (8 oz.) refrigerated crescent rolls
- 8 hot dogs
- 1 large egg, lightly beaten
- 1 Tbsp. water
- Caraway seeds

EQUIPMENT

- Baking sheet
- Bowl
- Fork
- Pastry brush

Make It Your Own!

MAKE THEM CHEESY. Give your piggies an extra blanket of cheese. Add a small slice of Swiss, cheddar or American cheese before rolling up the hot dogs in the dough.

SWITCH THE SEASONINGS. Some people don't like caraway seeds. You can omit them or substitute sesame seeds, poppy seeds or bagel seasoning on these dogs. Why not try a few of each?

GO FOR A DIP. Ketchup, honey mustard, barbecue sauce, cheesy queso dip and even chili are great options for dipping these piggies.

Cajun Popcorn Shrimp Sandwiches

You can adjust the heat level in these seafood sammies by tweaking the amount of seasoning and hot sauce. The mayonnaise mixture is a simple recipe for remoulade—a condiment that's popular in Cajun country. Use it for dipping french fries, fish sticks or hush puppies too.

—Kent Whitaker, Rossville, GA

TAKES: 30 min. • **MAKES:** 4 servings

INGREDIENTS

- 2 Tbsp. butter, melted
- 1 tsp. garlic powder
- ¼ to ½ tsp. Cajun seasoning
- 3½ cups frozen breaded popcorn shrimp
- ½ cup mayonnaise
- 1 Tbsp. hot pepper sauce
- 1 tsp. sweet pickle relish
- ½ tsp. prepared mustard
- 8 pita pocket halves, warmed
- 1 cup shredded lettuce
- 8 thin slices tomato

EQUIPMENT

- Bowls
- Measuring cups & spoons
- Kitchen spoon
- Baking pan
- Knife & cutting board

1. In a large bowl, combine butter, garlic powder and Cajun seasoning. Toss with shrimp. Prepare shrimp according to package directions for baking.

2. Combine the mayonnaise, pepper sauce, relish and mustard. Spread into warmed pitas. Fill pitas with shrimp, lettuce and tomato slices.

2 FILLED PITA HALVES 668 cal., 40g fat (8g sat. fat), 96mg chol., 1139mg sod., 58g carb. (5g sugars, 3g fiber), 18g pro.

The Game Plan

LITTLE KIDS CAN ...
Gather food and equipment, mix the remoulade and spread it into the pita pockets.

BIG KIDS CAN ...
Season and bake the shrimp, warm the pitas, prep the veggies and fill the pita pockets.

"This is going to be
good, I KNOW it …
Oh yeah, this is good!"
—COBY P., AGE 6

SKILL LEVEL **2**

Mac & Cheese Soup

I came across this recipe a few years ago and made some changes to suit my family's tastes. Because it starts with packaged macaroni and cheese, it's ready in a jiffy.
—Nancy Daugherty, Cortland, OH

TAKES: 30 min. • **MAKES:** 8 servings (2 qt.)

1. Set aside cheese sauce packet from macaroni and cheese mix. In a large saucepan, bring 8 cups water to a boil. Add macaroni; cook for 8-10 minutes or until tender.

2. Meanwhile, in another large saucepan, bring remaining 1 cup water to a boil. Add broccoli and onion; cook, uncovered, for 3 minutes. Stir in the soup, milk, ham and contents of cheese sauce packet; heat through. Drain macaroni; stir into soup.

1 CUP 263 cal., 9g fat (4g sat. fat), 28mg chol., 976mg sod., 32g carb. (6g sugars, 2g fiber), 13g pro.

Broccoli Mac & Cheese Soup Double the broccoli and omit the ham for a meatless option.

INGREDIENTS

- 1 pkg. (14 oz.) deluxe macaroni and cheese dinner mix
- 9 cups water, divided
- 1 cup fresh broccoli florets
- 2 Tbsp. finely chopped onion
- 1 can (10½ oz.) condensed cheddar cheese soup, undiluted
- 2½ cups 2% milk
- 1 cup chopped fully cooked ham

EQUIPMENT

- Large saucepans
- Measuring cup & spoon
- Kitchen spoon
- Knife & cutting board
- Strainer for cooked macaroni

Mac & Cheese Mix-Ins

You can make mac & cheese more hearty by stirring in sliced hot dogs or cooked Polish sausage, frozen mixed vegetables or cauliflowerets during the last few minutes of cooking. To make it richer, add bacon bits or shredded Monterey Jack cheese to the finished dish.

Coby P. has mac & cheese a few times per month. The secret to good macaroni is taste-testing it as you go, he says.

Cranberry Turkey Wraps

Fruity and flavorful, these grab-and-go wraps are quick to assemble and easy to handle.

—**Bobbie Keefer, Byers, CO**

TAKES: 15 min. • **MAKES:** 8 servings

INGREDIENTS

- 1 can (11 oz.) mandarin oranges, drained
- 1 medium tart apple, peeled and diced
- 3 Tbsp. dried cranberries
- ¾ cup fat-free plain yogurt
- 2 Tbsp. fat-free mayonnaise
- 8 flour tortillas (8 in.), warmed
- 8 lettuce leaves
- 1½ lbs. thinly sliced deli turkey
- 8 slices (1 oz. each) part-skim mozzarella cheese
- 2 Tbsp. chopped pecans, toasted

In a small bowl, combine the oranges, apple and cranberries. In another bowl, combine yogurt and mayonnaise; spread over tortillas. Layer each with lettuce, turkey, cheese, fruit mixture and pecans. Roll up tightly.

1 WRAP 374 cal., 12g fat (4g sat. fat), 54mg chol., 1477mg sod., 40g carb. (9g sugars, 1g fiber), 27g pro.

★★★★★

"Fabulous. Wouldn't change a thing. So bright and tasty."
—**VEERY, TASTEOFHOME.COM**

How to Roll an Easy-to-Eat Wrap

Place filling on the tortilla, leaving plenty of empty space around the edge. Fold in the left and right sides, then roll the tortilla up. The tucked-in ends keep ingredients from falling out of the wrap. This works for burritos too!

SKILL LEVEL 2

INGREDIENTS

- 1 **can (8 oz.) tomato sauce**
- 1 **cup chopped onion**
- 1 **cup barbecue sauce**
- 3 **tsp. chili powder**
- 1 **tsp. ground cumin**
- ½ **tsp. ground cinnamon**
- 1 **boneless pork sirloin roast (2 lbs.)**
- 8 **seeded hamburger buns, split**

    Optional: Sliced red onion, fresh cilantro leaves and dill pickle slices

EQUIPMENT

- 3-qt. slow cooker
- Knife & cutting board
- Measuring cup & spoons
- Kitchen spoon
- 2 forks

Pulled Pork from the Slow Cooker

You'll love the ease of this recipe—just throw everything in the slow cooker and get out of the kitchen. You hardly have to lift a finger for delicious results!
—**Terri McKitrick, Delafield, WI**

PREP: 15 min. • **COOK:** 7 hours • **MAKES:** 8 servings

1. In a 3-qt. slow cooker, combine the first 6 ingredients; add the pork. Spoon some of the sauce over pork. Cover and cook on low for 7 hours or until meat is tender.

2. Remove meat; shred with 2 forks. Return to slow cooker and heat through. Spoon ½ cup onto each bun. Serve with desired toppings.

1 SANDWICH 322 cal., 10g fat (3g sat. fat), 68mg chol., 681mg sod., 29g carb. (9g sugars, 3g fiber), 28g pro. **DIABETIC EXCHANGES** 3 lean meat, 2 starch.

> "One of my favorite meals! I have type 1 diabetes, and these sandwiches fit into my plan. I ask my mom for these all the time because they taste so good. My whole family likes them as much as I do!"
> **–IAN C., AGE 13**

SKILL LEVEL 1

Easy Chicken Ramen Bowl

From the first time I made this chicken dish, I knew it was a winner because the bowl came back to the kitchen scraped clean.
—Bess Blanco, Vail, AZ

TAKES: 15 min. • **MAKES:** 8 servings

Discard seasoning packet from noodles or save for another use. Break noodles into small pieces; place in a large bowl. Add chicken, coleslaw mix and green onions. Drizzle with salad dressing; toss to coat.

1½ CUPS 267 cal., 10g fat (3g sat. fat), 70mg chol., 405mg sod., 18g carb. (8g sugars, 2g fiber), 26g pro. **DIABETIC EXCHANGES** 3 lean meat, 1 starch, ½ fat.

INGREDIENTS

- 1 pkg. (3 oz.) ramen noodles
- 1 rotisserie chicken, skin removed, shredded
- 1 pkg. (16 oz.) coleslaw mix
- 6 green onions, finely chopped
- 1 cup reduced-fat Asian toasted sesame salad dressing

EQUIPMENT

- Large bowl
- Knife & cutting board
- Measuring cup
- Kitchen spoon

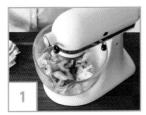  

How to Shred Chicken (3 Ways)

#1 STAND MIXER
Cut cooked chicken into chunks and add it to a stand mixer with the paddle attachment. A few seconds on medium-low speed is just enough to shred it.

#2 TWO FORKS
Use 2 large forks to pull cooked chicken into opposite directions.

#3 HANDS
After the chicken has cooled a little, pull it into shreds with your hands.

Looking Good.

To garnish this soup, we used mini food cutters to cut shapes from cheese slices. (You could use ham and veggies too.) Then we arranged the cutouts in snowflake designs on top of crackers.

SKILL LEVEL 2

Cozy Tomato Soup

Our sensational soup features lots of pleasing ingredients, and is extra fun to eat when decorated with pretty snowflakes.
—*Taste of Home* Test Kitchen

INGREDIENTS

- 2 cans (28 oz. each) crushed tomatoes
- 1 can (14½ oz.) chicken broth
- 2 Tbsp. minced fresh oregano or 2 tsp. dried oregano
- 1 to 2 Tbsp. sugar
- 1 cup heavy whipping cream

  Optional: Crackers and sliced white cheese

EQUIPMENT

- Blender
- Large saucepan
- Kitchen spoon
- Measuring cup & spoon

TAKES: 25 min. • **MAKES:** 10 servings (2½ qt.)

1. In a blender, process tomatoes, 1 can at a time, until smooth. Transfer to a large saucepan. Stir in the broth; bring to a boil. Reduce heat; cover and simmer for 10 minutes. Stir in oregano and sugar. Add a small amount of hot tomato mixture to whipping cream; return all to the saucepan. Cook, stirring often, until soup is slightly thickened (do not boil).

2. If desired, cut snowflake shapes from sliced cheese using small cutter; arrange on top of crackers. Place soup into serving bowl; top with crackers and cheese if desired.

1 CUP 140 cal., 9g fat (6g sat. fat), 27mg chol., 451mg sod., 14g carb. (9g sugars, 3g fiber), 3g pro.

Silly Tortilla Mustaches

Cut four **8-in. flour tortillas** with kitchen shears to form 8 mustaches; discard scraps. Brush both sides of cutouts with **melted butter**; place on an ungreased baking sheet. Combine ½ tsp. **dried basil**, ½ tsp. **dried thyme**, ¼ tsp. **seasoned salt**, ¼ tsp. **garlic powder** and ½ tsp. **pepper**; sprinkle over mustaches. Bake at 400° for 5-7 minutes or until crisp. Use to decorate soup bowls with **cooked wagon wheel pasta** and **Goldfish crackers**.

SKILL LEVEL 1

Creamy Fruit Salad with Yogurt

Kids can't wait to eat this refreshing salad ... I know ours can't! It's healthy and simple to make, and tastes great. Our family can't get enough of it.

—Lisa Dunn, Red Oak, OK

TAKES: 15 min. • **MAKES:** 6 servings

INGREDIENTS

- 1 **can (15 oz.) fruit cocktail, undrained**
- 2 **medium firm bananas, sliced**
- 1 **medium apple, chopped**
- 1 **medium navel orange, peeled and cut into sections**
- 2 **Tbsp. instant vanilla pudding mix**
- 1 **cup vanilla yogurt**

EQUIPMENT

- **Bowls**
- **Knife & cutting board**
- **Measuring cup & spoon**
- **Kitchen spoon**

In a serving bowl, combine fruit cocktail, bananas, apple and orange. Combine pudding mix and yogurt until smooth. Add to fruit mixture; stir to coat. Refrigerate leftovers.

¾ CUP 156 cal., 1g fat (0 sat. fat), 2mg chol., 51mg sod., 37g carb. (30g sugars, 3g fiber), 3g pro.

Instant Apple Slices

Cut an apple into wedges, then put it back together again. Secure with a rubber band and pop it in your lunch. Add a little container of caramel sauce or peanut butter for dipping.

"Fruit salads
are the best!"
–ABIGAIL P., AGE 5

INGREDIENTS

- 1 pkg. (11¼ oz.) frozen garlic Texas toast
- ¼ cup pasta sauce
- 4 slices provolone cheese
- 16 slices pepperoni
- 8 slices thinly sliced hard salami
-   Additional pasta sauce, warmed, optional

EQUIPMENT

- Griddle or large skillet
- Turner
- Measuring spoon

Garlic Bread Pizza Sandwiches

I love inventing new ways to make grilled cheese sandwiches for my kids. This version tastes like pizza. Using frozen garlic bread is a timesaver.
—Courtney Stultz, Weir, KS

TAKES: 20 min. • **MAKES:** 4 servings

1. Preheat griddle over medium-low heat. Add garlic toast; cook until lightly browned, 3-4 minutes per side.

2. Spoon 1 Tbsp. sauce over each of 4 pieces of toast. Top with cheese, pepperoni, salami and remaining toast. Cook until crisp and cheese is melted, 3-5 minutes, turning as necessary. If desired, serve with additional sauce.

1 SANDWICH 456 cal., 28g fat (10g sat. fat), 50mg chol., 1177mg sod., 36g carb. (4g sugars, 2g fiber), 19g pro.

"I substituted pizza sauce for the pasta sauce because that's what I had on hand. Using the garlic bread gave this an extra flavor boost. So simple and yummy for a cold night."
—CUPCAKE_K9, TASTEOFHOME.COM

SKILL LEVEL
2

Farmhouse Barbecue Muffins

Tangy barbecue sauce, fluffy biscuits and cheddar cheese combine to make these hand-held lunches. Try them with ground turkey or other shredded cheeses to vary the flavor.

—Karen Kenney, Harvard, IL

INGREDIENTS

- 1 tube (12 oz.) refrigerated buttermilk biscuits
- 1 lb. ground beef
- ½ cup ketchup
- 3 Tbsp. brown sugar
- 1 Tbsp. cider vinegar
- ½ tsp. chili powder
- 1 cup shredded cheddar cheese

EQUIPMENT

- Rolling pin
- Ruler
- Muffin tin
- Large skillet
- Kitchen spoon
- Strainer for cooked beef
- Small bowl
- Measuring cups & spoons

PREP: 20 min. • **BAKE:** 20 min. • **MAKES:** 10 servings

1. Separate dough into 10 biscuits; with a rolling pin, flatten into 5-in. circles. Press each onto the bottom and up the side of a greased muffin cup; set aside.

2. In a large skillet, cook beef over medium heat until no longer pink, 5-7 minutes, crumbling the beef; drain. In a small bowl, combine the ketchup, brown sugar, vinegar and chili powder; add to beef and mix well.

3. Divide the meat mixture among biscuit-lined muffin cups, using about ¼ cup for each. Sprinkle with cheese. Bake at 375° for 18-20 minutes or until golden brown. Cool for 5 minutes before serving.

1 MUFFIN 226 cal., 9 g fat (5 g sat. fat), 42 mg chol., 477 mg sod., 21 g carb., trace fiber, 14 g pro.

How to Press Dough into Muffin Tins

Press a dough circle evenly onto the bottom of each muffin cup, then against the side. If the dough comes above the muffin cups, make sure the dough cups do not touch one another.

SKILL LEVEL 1

INGREDIENTS

- ⅔ cup mayonnaise
- ½ cup dill pickle relish
- 1 Tbsp. minced fresh parsley
- 1 tsp. lemon juice
- ½ tsp. seasoned salt
- ⅛ tsp. pepper
- 2 cups cubed cooked chicken
- 1 cup cubed Swiss cheese
- 6 croissants, split
- Lettuce leaves

EQUIPMENT

- Bowl
- Measuring cups & spoons
- Knife & cutting board
- Kitchen spoon

Chicken Salad Croissants

This chicken salad gets its unique taste from Swiss cheese and relish. It's my brother's favorite. I make it every time he visits.

—Laura Koziarski, Battle Creek, MI

TAKES: 15 min. • **MAKES:** 6 servings

Mix first 6 ingredients; stir in chicken and cheese. Serve on croissants lined with lettuce.

1 SANDWICH 593 cal., 40g fat (14g sat. fat), 102mg chol., 818mg sod., 33g carb. (6g sugars, 2g fiber), 24g pro.

"Family favorite. Lately we have been putting it on heavier artisan breads, like sourdough, and then grilling it. The melted Swiss cheese adds a bit of nutty taste to the salad. Amazing!"

—LADYDRAGONFLY, TASTEOFHOME.COM

SKILL LEVEL 2

INGREDIENTS

2 qt. water

8 tsp. chicken bouillon granules

6½ cups uncooked wide egg noodles

2 cans (10¾ oz. each) condensed cream of chicken soup, undiluted

3 cups cubed cooked chicken

1 cup sour cream

Minced fresh parsley

EQUIPMENT

- Large saucepan
- Measuring cups & spoon
- Kitchen spoon
- Knife & cutting board

Comforting Chicken Noodle Soup

A good friend made us this rich, comforting soup after our son was born. It was such a help to have dinner taken care of until I was back on my feet. This yummy dish is so simple to fix that now I give a pot of it (along with the recipe) to other new moms.

—Joanna Sargent, Sandy, UT

TAKES: 25 min. • **MAKES:** 12 servings (3 qt.)

1. In a large saucepan, bring water and bouillon to a boil. Add noodles; cook, uncovered, until tender, about 10 minutes. Do not drain. Add soup and chicken; heat through.

2. Remove from the heat; stir in the sour cream. Sprinkle with minced parsley.

1 CUP 218 cal., 9g fat (4g sat. fat), 67mg chol., 980mg sod., 18g carb. (2g sugars, 1g fiber), 15g pro.

How to Keep Parsley Fresh

Trim the stems and place parsley in a glass with an inch of water. Be sure no leaves are in the water. Tie a produce bag around the glass to trap humidity; store in the refrigerator. Each time you use the parsley, change the water and turn the produce bag inside out. This releases any moisture that built up inside the bag. You can keep parsley fresh for up to a month this way.

SKILL LEVEL 1

INGREDIENTS

- ¼ cup creamy peanut butter
- 2 Tbsp. honey
- ¼ tsp. ground cinnamon
- 2 Tbsp. miniature semisweet chocolate chips
- 4 slices whole wheat bread
- 1 medium banana, thinly sliced

EQUIPMENT

- Small bowl
- Measuring cup & spoons
- Kitchen spoon
- Butter knife
- Knife & cutting board

Chocolate Chip, PB & Banana Sandwiches

I love finding new ways to combine peanut butter, chocolate and bananas. I was shocked when my nephews (who are very picky eaters) loved these sammies.

—Charlotte Gehle, Brownstown, MI

TAKES: 10 min. • **MAKES:** 2 servings

Mix peanut butter, honey and cinnamon; stir in chocolate chips. Spread over bread. Layer 2 bread slices with banana slices; top with remaining bread. If desired, cut into shapes using cookie cutters.

1 SANDWICH 502 cal., 22g fat (6g sat. fat), 0 chol., 394mg sod., 69g carb. (36g sugars, 7g fiber), 15g pro.

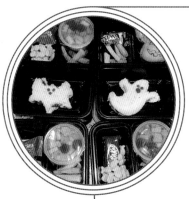

Spooktacular Lunch Preps

"These cheap divided containers fit perfectly into my kids' lunchboxes. They keep stuff fresh and protected, but cut down on packaging. I do all the meal prepping on Sunday, so the lunches are ready and in the fridge all week." —Andrea K., mom

Andrea and Sophia K. make bat- and ghost-shaped sandwiches for Halloween. All-orange foods, such as peaches, Goldfish crackers and baby carrots, carry the theme.

"I help Mom make lunches for school. I count baby carrots and apple slices and put them in the containers."

—SOPHIA K., AGE 5

PAGE
113

FAMILY-FAVORITE DINNERS

Mini Meat Loaves

Serve these tangy meat loaf muffins for dinner or slice them up to put in sandwiches. They're just as flavorful after freezing.

—Cheryl Norwood, Canton, GA

TAKES: 30 min. • **MAKES:** 6 servings

INGREDIENTS

- 1 **large egg, lightly beaten**
- ½ **cup dry bread crumbs**
- ½ **cup finely chopped onion**
- ½ **cup finely chopped green pepper**
- ¼ **cup barbecue sauce**
- 1½ **lbs. lean ground beef (90% lean)**
- 3 **Tbsp. ketchup**

  Additional ketchup, optional

EQUIPMENT

- **Bowl**
- **Measuring cups & spoon**
- **Knife & cutting board**
- **Muffin tin**
- **Pastry brush**
- **Thermometer**

1. Preheat oven to 375°. In a bowl, mix the first 5 ingredients. Add beef; mix lightly but thoroughly. Press about ⅓ cupful into each of 12 ungreased muffin cups.

2. Bake 15 minutes. Brush tops of loaves with 3 Tbsp. ketchup; bake 5-7 minutes or until a thermometer reads 160°. If desired, serve with additional ketchup.

FREEZE OPTION Bake muffins without ketchup; cover and freeze on a waxed paper-lined baking sheet until firm. Transfer muffins to an airtight freezer container; return to freezer. To use, partially thaw in refrigerator overnight. Place muffins on a greased shallow baking pan. Spread with ketchup. Bake in a preheated 350° oven until heated through.

2 MINI MEAT LOAVES 260 cal., 11g fat (4g sat. fat), 102mg chol., 350mg sod., 15g carb. (7g sugars, 1g fiber), 24g pro.

Make It Your Own!

Put a surprise inside! Tuck a mozzarella cheese pearl or cube of cheddar cheese into each uncooked meat loaf. If you like a sweeter topping, mix the ketchup with 1 Tbsp. packed brown sugar before brushing on top of the loaves.

EQUIPMENT

- Bowls
- Measuring cups & spoons
- Whisk
- Knife & cutting board
- Kitchen spoon

SKILL LEVEL 1

ABC Salad Toss

Getting your share of veggies, fruit and protein is as easy as ABC—that's apples, bananas and cheese. This slightly sweet salad appeals to your taste buds while still delivering lots of healthy benefits.
—**Christine Maddux, Council Blfs, IA**

TAKES: 25 min. • **MAKES:** 16 servings

INGREDIENTS

- 1 pkg. (12 oz.) broccoli coleslaw mix
- 1 pkg. (8 oz.) ready-to-serve salad greens
- ½ cup mayonnaise
- 1 Tbsp. sugar
- 2 tsp. olive oil
- 8 oz. Colby-Monterey Jack cheese, cut into ½-in. cubes
- 1 medium apple, chopped
- 1 cup seedless red grapes, halved
- ¼ cup raisins
- 1 medium banana, sliced

In a large bowl, combine coleslaw mix and salad greens. Whisk together mayonnaise, sugar and oil; stir in cheese, apple, grapes and raisins. Pour over salad; toss to coat. Top with banana slices. Serve immediately.

1 CUP 143 cal., 10g fat (4g sat. fat), 14mg chol., 135mg sod., 10g carb. (6g sugars, 1g fiber), 4g pro.

How to Toss Salad

After combining salad greens in a bowl, add sturdy ingredients like cheese cubes, fresh fruit or meats. Drizzle dressing over salad and mix with a kitchen spoon. Stir ingredients up from the bottom to cover evenly with dressing. Top the salad with fragile ingredients, such as sliced banana, egg or avocado.

SKILL LEVEL 3

Pan Burritos

Our family loves Mexican food, so this flavorful, satisfying casserole is a favorite. It's nice to get the taste of burritos while cutting any serving size you want.

—Joyce Kent, Grand Rapids, MI

PREP: 35 min. • **BAKE:** 35 min. + standing • **MAKES:** 10 servings

INGREDIENTS

- 2 pkg. (1½ oz. each) enchilada sauce mix
- 3 cups water
- 1 can (12 oz.) tomato paste
- 1 garlic clove, minced
- ¼ tsp. pepper
  Salt to taste
- 2 lbs. ground beef
- 9 large flour tortillas (9 in.)
- 4 cups shredded cheddar cheese or Mexican cheese blend
- 1 can (16 oz.) refried beans, warmed
  Optional: Taco sauce, sour cream, chile peppers, chopped onion and guacamole

EQUIPMENT

- Large saucepan
- Measuring cups & spoon
- Large skillet
- Strainer for cooked meat
- Kitchen spoons
- 13x9-in. baking pan or dish
- Spatula

1. In a large saucepan, combine the first 6 ingredients; simmer for 15-20 minutes.

2. In a large skillet, brown and crumble the beef. Drain; stir in a third of the sauce. Spread another third on the bottom of a greased 13x9-in. baking pan or dish.

3. Place 3 tortillas over sauce, tearing to fit the bottom of pan. Spoon half of the meat mixture over tortillas; sprinkle with 1½ cups cheese. Add 3 more tortillas. Spread refried beans over tortillas with a spatula; top with remaining meat. Sprinkle with 1½ cups of cheese. Layer with remaining tortillas and remaining sauce. Sprinkle with remaining 1 cup cheese.

4. Bake, uncovered, at 350° until heated through, 35-40 minutes. Let stand for 10 minutes before cutting. Serve with the optional ingredients as desired.

1 PIECE 646 cal., 32g fat (15g sat. fat), 101mg chol., 1379mg sod., 52g carb. (7g sugars, 5g fiber), 36g pro.

"I made it for my daughter's birthday. She loves Mexican food. This recipe was a big hit with her and the entire family! I used taco seasoning instead of enchilada sauce mix, and it was great. It wasn't too spicy."

—DJBYRD2, TASTEOFHOME.COM

How to Brown Ground Beef

STEP 1: Heat a large skillet over medium heat, then crumble meat into the pan. After a few minutes, use a kitchen spoon to break up the larger chunks of meat and gently stir it around.

STEP 2: Cook until meat is no longer pink, then drain. (Techniques vary for this; ask an adult for guidance.)

SKILL LEVEL **2**

INGREDIENTS

- 1 pkg. (16.3 oz.) large refrigerated buttermilk biscuits
- 1 cup shredded part-skim mozzarella cheese
- 24 slices turkey pepperoni (about 1½ oz.)
- 2 ready-to-serve fully cooked bacon strips, chopped

  Pizza sauce, warmed

EQUIPMENT

- Rolling pin
- Waffle maker
- Measuring cup
- Knife & cutting board

Waffle-Maker Pizzas

These little pizza pockets put together using the waffle maker are a fun mashup. Try your favorite toppings or even breakfast fillings like ham and eggs.

—Amy Lents, Grand Forks, ND

TAKES: 30 min. • **MAKES:** 4 servings

1. Roll or press biscuits to fit waffle maker. On 1 biscuit, place ¼ cup cheese, 6 slices pepperoni and a fourth of the chopped bacon to within ½ in. of edges. Top with a second biscuit, folding bottom edge over top edge and pressing to seal completely.

2. Bake in a preheated waffle maker according to manufacturer's directions until golden brown, 4-5 minutes. Repeat with the remaining ingredients. Serve with pizza sauce.

1 PIZZA 461 cal., 21g fat (8g sat. fat), 28mg chol., 1650mg sod., 50g carb. (5g sugars, 2g fiber), 19g pro.

★★★★★

"My son had a blast helping me put together these little pizza pockets. So much fun for our pizza-themed Fridays. We'll definitely do it again!"

—ANGEL182009, TASTEOFHOME.COM

SKILL LEVEL **2**

INGREDIENTS

2 Tbsp. butter, melted

1 cup crushed cornflakes

1 cup all-purpose flour

1½ tsp. seasoned salt

¾ cup egg substitute or 3 large eggs, beaten

4 chicken drumsticks (4 oz. each), skin removed

4 bone-in chicken thighs (about 1½ lbs.), skin removed

EQUIPMENT

- 13x9-in. baking dish
- Shallow bowls
- Measuring cups & spoons
- Thermometer

Cornflake "Fried" Chicken

I took a recipe off a box of baking mix and altered it to make the prep easier. The result was this moist oven-fried chicken with a thick golden coating that's a lot more crispy than the original.

—Angela Capettini,
 Boynton Beach, FL

PREP: 10 min. • **BAKE:** 30 min. • **MAKES:** 4 servings

1. Preheat oven to 425°. Drizzle butter in a 13x9-in. baking dish. In a shallow bowl, combine cornflakes, flour and seasoned salt. Place egg substitute in another shallow bowl. Dip chicken in egg substitute, then roll in cornflake mixture. Repeat.

2. Arrange chicken in prepared dish, meatier side down. Bake, uncovered, 20 minutes. Turn chicken over; bake 10-15 minutes longer or until a thermometer reads 170°-175°.

1 DRUMSTICK AND 1 THIGH 534 cal., 18g fat (7g sat. fat), 143mg chol., 972mg sod., 44g carb. (3g sugars, 1g fiber), 46g pro.

Breading chicken in wet, then dry ingredients is a good job for two people. If working alone, use one hand for the egg mixture and the other for the crumbs. You'll have an easier time washing up when you're finished.

How to Shape Meatballs

If you're handy with a scoop, you can use it to quickly shape meatballs. Whatever you use, try to make yours all the same size. Large meatballs take longer to cook than small ones.

SKILL LEVEL 2

INGREDIENTS

- ½ cup uncooked long grain rice
- ½ cup water
- ⅓ cup chopped onion
- 1 tsp. salt
- ½ tsp. celery salt
- ⅛ tsp. pepper
- ⅛ tsp. garlic powder
- 1 lb. ground beef
- 2 Tbsp. canola oil
- 1 can (15 oz.) tomato sauce
- 1 cup water
- 2 Tbsp. brown sugar
- 2 tsp. Worcestershire sauce

  Chopped green onions, optional

EQUIPMENT

- Bowls
- Measuring cups & spoons
- Knife & cutting board
- Kitchen spoon
- Large skillet with lid
- Strainer for cooked meatballs

Porcupine Meatballs

These meatballs in a rich tomato sauce are one of my mom's best dishes. I used to love this meal when I was growing up. I made it at home for our children, and now my daughters make it for their families.

—Darlis Wilfer, West Bend, WI

PREP: 20 min. • **COOK:** 1 hour • **MAKES:** 4 servings

1. In a bowl, combine the first 7 ingredients. Add beef and mix well. Shape into 1½-in. balls.

2. In a large skillet, brown meatballs in oil; drain. Combine the tomato sauce, water, brown sugar and Worcestershire sauce; pour over meatballs. Reduce heat; cover and simmer for 1 hour. If desired, sprinkle with green onions.

1 SERVING 421 cal., 21g fat (6g sat. fat), 70mg chol., 1317mg sod., 34g carb. (9g sugars, 2g fiber), 24g pro.

> **"Meatballs and rice is one of my favorite foods. I eat a lot so I can get stronger, and that's good."**
> **–ELIAS F., AGE 6**

INGREDIENTS

2¾ to 3 cups all-purpose
    flour

1 pkg. (¼ oz.) active
    dry yeast

¼ tsp. salt

1 cup warm water
    (120° to 130°)

1 Tbsp. canola oil

SAUCE

1 can (14½ oz.) diced
    tomatoes, undrained

1 can (6 oz.) tomato
    paste

1 Tbsp. canola oil

1 tsp. salt

½ tsp. each dried basil,
    oregano, marjoram
    and thyme

¼ tsp. garlic powder

¼ tsp. pepper

PIZZAS

1 pkg. (3½ oz.) sliced
    pepperoni

5 cups shredded part-
    skim mozzarella
    cheese

¼ cup grated Parmesan
    cheese

¼ cup grated Romano
    cheese

Pepperoni Pan Pizzas

I've spent years trying to come up with the perfect pizza crust and sauce, and they're paired up in this recipe. I fix this crispy pizza for my family often, and it really satisfies my husband and three sons.

—Susan Lindahl, Alford, FL

PREP: 30 min. + standing • **BAKE:** 10 min. • **MAKES:** 2 pizzas (9 pieces each)

1. In a large bowl, combine 2 cups flour, yeast and salt. Add water and oil; beat until smooth. Add enough remaining flour to form a soft dough.

2. Turn onto a floured surface; knead until smooth and elastic, 5-7 minutes. Cover and let stand for 10 minutes. Meanwhile, in a small bowl, combine tomatoes, tomato paste, oil and seasonings.

3. Divide dough in half; press into two 15x10x1-in. baking pans coated with cooking spray. Prick dough generously with a fork. Bake at 425° until lightly browned, 12-16 minutes.

4. Spread sauce over crusts; top with pepperoni and cheeses. Bake until cheese is melted, 8-10 minutes. Cut into squares.

FREEZE OPTION Bake crusts and assemble pizzas as directed. Securely wrap and freeze unbaked pizzas. To use, unwrap pizzas; bake as directed, increasing time as necessary.

2 PIECES 460 cal., 23g fat (10g sat. fat), 56mg chol., 1096mg sod., 39g carb. (4g sugars, 3g fiber), 25g pro.

Make It Your Own!

To create a classic Hawaiian pizza, top the pizza sauce with chopped Canadian bacon and well-drained pineapple tidbits. Then top with cheeses.

EQUIPMENT

- Bowls
- Measuring cups & spoons
- Kitchen spoon
- Two 15x10x1-in. baking pans
- Fork

SKILL LEVEL
2

Fancy Baked Ham

I can still picture the table set perfectly at our 150-year-old family farm, and I can almost smell the ham baking! Every time I cook this ham, I think of my mom—she was the best cook ever!

—Rosemary Pryor, Pasadena, MD

INGREDIENTS

- 1 can (8 oz.) sliced pineapple
- 1 canned ham (5 lbs.)
- ½ cup packed brown sugar
- 1 tsp. ground mustard
- ¼ tsp. ground cloves
- 1 Tbsp. cider vinegar
  Maraschino cherries

EQUIPMENT

- Baking dish
- Small bowl
- Measuring cup and spoons
- Knife
- Spoon
- Thermometer

PREP: 10 min. • **BAKE:** 70 min. • **MAKES:** 10 servings

1. Drain pineapple, reserving 2 Tbsp. juice; set aside. Place ham in a baking dish. Bake at 350° for 30 minutes.

2. In a small bowl, combine brown sugar, mustard, cloves, vinegar and reserved pineapple juice. Score top of ham. Place pineapple slices and cherries over ham; spoon glaze over top.

3. Bake 40-45 minutes longer or until a thermometer reads 140°, basting occasionally.

6 OZ. HAM 296 cal., 8g fat (3g sat. fat), 116mg chol., 2357mg sod., 14g carb. (14g sugars, 0 fiber), 42g pro.

The Game Plan

LITTLE KIDS CAN ...
Gather food and equipment, drain the pineapple, mix the glaze and blot the cherries.

BIG KIDS CAN ...
Score and bake ham, arrange fruits and top with glaze.

SKILL LEVEL 2

Bean & Cheese Quesadillas

My son doesn't eat meat, so I created this recipe as a way for me to cook one meal for the family instead of two. It's so easy that my toddler grandson helps me make it!
—**Tina McMullen, Salina, KS**

INGREDIENTS

- 1 can (16 oz.) refried beans
- ½ cup canned petite diced tomatoes
- 2 green onions, chopped
- 12 flour tortillas (8 in.)
- 2 cups shredded cheddar cheese

  Optional: Sour cream and salsa

EQUIPMENT

- Small bowl
- Measuring cup
- Knife & cutting board
- Spatula
- Griddle or large skillet

TAKES: 30 min. • **MAKES:** 6 servings

1. In a small bowl, mix beans, tomatoes and green onions. Spread half of the tortillas with bean mixture. Sprinkle with cheese; top with remaining tortillas.

2. Heat a griddle over medium heat. Place tortillas on griddle in batches. Cook for 2-3 minutes on each side or until golden brown and cheese is melted. If desired, serve with sour cream and salsa.

1 QUESADILLA 544 cal., 21g fat (9g sat. fat), 37mg chol., 1028mg sod., 67g carb. (1g sugars, 6g fiber), 21g pro.

Bacon-Tomato Quesadillas Use 8 medium tomatoes, seeded and finely chopped; 8 bacon strips, cooked and crumbled; and 3 cups (12 oz.) shredded Mexican cheese blend instead of the first 3 ingredients. Omit cheddar cheese. Assemble and cook as directed.

How to Save a Cutting Board

Use kitchen shears for little jobs like snipping green onions or fresh herbs. Then you won't have to wash a cutting board.

SKILL LEVEL 1

Sheet-Pan Steak Dinner

Asparagus and steak are a yummy pair for dinner. Cooking them together is easy and makes cleanup quicker. In our house, we love meals that cook in the oven while we finish up other things!

—Pamela Forrest, Springfield, OR

PREP: 15 min. • **BAKE:** 25 min. • **MAKES:** 4 servings

INGREDIENTS

- 1 tsp. minced fresh rosemary
- ½ tsp. each salt, pepper, paprika and garlic powder
- 1½ lbs. beef flank steak
- 1 lb. fresh asparagus, trimmed
- 2 Tbsp. avocado or vegetable oil
- 2 Tbsp. butter, melted
- 1 garlic clove, minced

EQUIPMENT

- Small bowls
- Measuring spoons
- 15x10x1-in. baking pan
- Brush
- Knife & cutting board
- Thermometer

1. Preheat oven to 400°. In a small bowl, combine rosemary and seasonings; set aside.

2. Place steak on 1 side of a 15x10x1-in. baking pan; place asparagus on other side in a single layer. Brush steak with oil and sprinkle with seasoning mix. Combine butter and garlic; pour over asparagus.

3. Cover with foil; bake 25-30 minutes or until meat reaches desired doneness (for medium-rare, a thermometer should read 135°; medium, 140°; medium-well, 145°). Let steak stand for 5-10 minutes before slicing. Serve with asparagus.

5 OZ. COOKED BEEF WITH 8 ASPARAGUS SPEARS 380 cal., 25g fat (10g sat. fat), 96mg chol., 448mg sod., 3g carb. (1g sugars, 1g fiber), 34g pro.

How to Cut Meat

Hold a knife in the hand you write with. Hold meat steady with a fork in your other hand. Cut meat across the grain. If you cut it *with* the grain, you'll get stringy fibers that are harder to chew.

How to Prep Asparagus

STEP 1: After rinsing, bend each stalk near the bottom. The stalk will break at the tough part, which is not as tasty and tender as the rest. Discard this tough portion.

STEP 2: If stalks are large, use a vegetable peeler to remove the tough outer stems.

"Pizza should be its own food group."

—GERARDO S., AGE 9

SKILL LEVEL 3

Pizza on a Stick

My daughter and her friends had fun turning sausage, pepperoni, veggies and pizza dough into these cute kabobs.
—**Charlene Woods, Norfolk, VA**

TAKES: 30 min. • **MAKES:** 5 servings

INGREDIENTS

- 8 oz. Italian turkey sausage links
- 2 cups whole fresh mushrooms
- 2 cups cherry tomatoes
- 1 medium onion, cut into 1-in. pieces
- 1 large green pepper, cut into 1-in. pieces
- 30 slices turkey pepperoni (2 oz.)
- 1 tube (13.8 oz.) refrigerated pizza crust
- 1½ cups shredded part-skim mozzarella cheese
- 1¼ cups pizza sauce, warmed

EQUIPMENT

- Large nonstick skillet
- Tongs
- Knife & cutting board
- 10 metal or wooden skewers
- Ruler
- Baking sheet

1. Preheat oven to 400°. In a large nonstick skillet, cook sausage over medium heat until it is no longer pink, turning with tongs occasionally; drain. When cool enough to handle, cut sausage into 20 pieces. On 10 metal or wooden skewers, alternately thread sausage, vegetables and pepperoni.

2. Unroll pizza dough onto a lightly floured surface; cut widthwise into 1-in.-wide strips. Starting at the pointed end of a prepared skewer, pierce skewer through 1 end of dough strip. Spiral-wrap dough strip around skewer, allowing vegetables and meats to peek through. Wrap remaining end of dough strip around skewer above the first ingredient. Repeat with remaining dough strips and skewers.

3. Arrange kabobs on a baking sheet coated with cooking spray. Bake for 10-12 minutes or until vegetables are tender and pizza crust is golden. Immediately sprinkle with cheese. Serve with pizza sauce.

2 KABOBS WITH ¼ CUP SAUCE 429 cal., 15g fat (6g sat. fat), 52mg chol., 1337mg sod., 52g carb. (13g sugars, 3g fiber), 26g pro.

"I made these with my granddaughter, and it was fun. We used frozen Italian meatballs, thawed, instead of the sausage. She absolutely loved them."
—**EBRAMKAMP, TASTEOFHOME.COM**

SKILL LEVEL 3

INGREDIENTS

- 1 **sheet refrigerated pie crust**
- ¾ **lb. ground beef**
- 2 **plum tomatoes, seeded and chopped**
- 1 **medium onion, chopped**
- ½ **cup dill pickle relish**
- ½ **cup crumbled cooked bacon**
- 5 **large eggs**
- 1 **cup heavy cream**
- ½ **cup 2% milk**
- 2 **tsp. prepared mustard**
- 1 **tsp. hot pepper sauce**
- ½ **tsp. salt**
- ¼ **tsp. pepper**
- 1½ **cups shredded cheddar cheese**
- ½ **cup shredded Parmesan cheese**

EQUIPMENT

- 9-in. deep-dish pie plate
- Large skillet
- Kitchen spoon
- Strainer for cooked beef
- Knife & cutting board
- Measuring cups & spoons
- Large bowl

Roadside Diner Cheeseburger Quiche

Here is an unforgettable quiche that tastes just like its burger counterpart. Easy and appealing, it's perfect for guests and fun for the whole family.
—Barbara J. Miller, Oakdale, MN

PREP: 20 min. • **BAKE:** 50 min. + standing • **MAKES:** 8 servings

1. Preheat oven to 375°. Unroll crust into a 9-in. deep-dish pie plate; flute edges. In a large skillet, cook beef over medium heat until no longer pink, breaking it into crumbles; drain. Stir in tomatoes, onion, relish and bacon. Transfer to prepared crust.

2. In a large bowl, mix eggs, cream, milk, mustard, pepper sauce, salt and pepper. Pour over beef mixture. Sprinkle with cheeses.

3. Bake 50-60 minutes or until a knife inserted in center comes out clean. If necessary, cover edges with foil during the last 15 minutes to prevent overbrowning. Let stand for 10 minutes before cutting.

1 PIECE 502 cal., 35g fat (19g sat. fat), 236mg chol., 954mg sod., 24g carb. (8g sugars, 1g fiber), 23g pro.

Make It Your Own!

Serve the quiche with your fave burger toppings such as mayonnaise, pickles, crumbled cooked bacon, ketchup, lettuce leaves and chopped tomato. Serve it with hash brown patties or french fries and smoothies or milkshakes.

How to Flute a Pie Crust

Put your index finger on the edge of the crust, pointing outward. Then place the thumb and index finger of your other hand on the outside of the edge and pinch towards your finger, forming a "V" shape. Continue around the entire edge. It doesn't have to be perfect. The only important thing is that the pie crust doesn't have any holes where liquid egg can leak underneath.

SKILL LEVEL 1

Baked Lemon Haddock

After testing out lots of haddock recipes, I've decided this baked version is the best. The mix of crunchy topping and lemon is just delicious.

—Jean Ann Perkins, Newburyport, MA

INGREDIENTS

- 2 lbs. haddock fillets
- 1 cup seasoned dry bread crumbs
- ¼ cup butter, melted
- 2 Tbsp. dried parsley flakes
- 2 tsp. grated lemon zest
- ½ tsp. garlic powder

EQUIPMENT

- Knife & cutting board
- 11x7-in. baking dish
- Small bowl
- Measuring cup & spoons
- Zesting tool

TAKES: 30 min. • **MAKES:** 6 servings

Preheat oven to 350°. Cut fish into 6 serving-sized pieces. Place in a greased 11x7-in. baking dish. In a small bowl, combine the remaining ingredients; sprinkle over fish. Bake until fish just begins to flake easily with a fork, 20-25 minutes.

4 OZ. COOKED FISH 269 cal., 9g fat (5g sat. fat), 108mg chol., 446mg sod., 13g carb. (1g sugars, 1g fiber), 32g pro. **DIABETIC EXCHANGES** 4 lean meat, 2 fat, 1 starch.

1

2

How to Zest a Lemon (2 Ways)

#1 RASP
Our favorite way is with a rasp, a hand-held grater that makes ready-to-use, superfine zest.

#2 BOX GRATER
Using the finest side of a box grater is another technique. Be careful not to grate too far down through the peel, as the pale-colored pith tastes bitter.

SKILL LEVEL 2

Meatless Chili Mac

I came across this recipe in a newspaper years ago. It's been a hit at our house ever since. It's fast and flavorful, and it appeals to all ages.

—Cindy Ragan,
North Huntingdon, PA

PREP: 15 min. • **COOK:** 25 min. • **MAKES:** 8 servings

INGREDIENTS

- 1 **large onion, chopped**
- 1 **medium green pepper, chopped**
- 1 **Tbsp. olive oil**
- 1 **garlic clove, minced**
- 2 **cups water**
- 1½ **cups uncooked elbow macaroni**
- 1 **can (16 oz.) mild chili beans, undrained**
- 1 **can (15½ oz.) great northern beans, rinsed and drained**
- 1 **can (14½ oz.) diced tomatoes, undrained**
- 1 **can (8 oz.) tomato sauce**
- 4 **tsp. chili powder**
- 1 **tsp. ground cumin**
- ½ **tsp. salt**
- ½ **cup fat-free sour cream**

EQUIPMENT

- **Dutch oven**
- **Knife & cutting board**
- **Measuring cups & spoons**
- **Kitchen spoon**

1. In a Dutch oven, saute onion and green pepper in oil until tender. Add garlic; cook 1 minute longer. Stir in water, macaroni, beans, tomatoes, tomato sauce, chili powder, cumin and salt.

2. Bring to a boil. Reduce heat; cover and simmer until macaroni is tender, 15-20 minutes. Top each serving with 1 Tbsp. sour cream.

1¼ CUPS 206 cal., 3g fat (1g sat. fat), 1mg chol., 651mg sod., 37g carb. (6g sugars, 9g fiber), 10g pro. **DIABETIC EXCHANGES** 2 starch, 1 vegetable, 1 lean meat.

Did You Know?

Beans really are the magical fruit. They're packed with protein and fiber, so you feel full for a long time after eating them. Since they don't use as many resources to grow as animals do, eating them is good for the environment too. (You can also add beans to meat-containing dishes and feed more people for not a lot of money.)

If you want to toot less after eating beans, be sure to rinse them well before cooking, chew the beans slowly and introduce them gradually into your diet.

"Best casserole ever."
—ISABELLE P., AGE 7

SKILL LEVEL
2

Tater-Topped Casserole

I grew up enjoying this dish. My mother always saw smiles around the table whenever she served it!

—Victoria Mitchell, Salem, VA

PREP: 15 min. • **BAKE:** 45 min. • **MAKES:** 6 servings

INGREDIENTS

- 1   lb. lean ground beef (90% lean)
- ½ cup chopped onion
- ⅓ cup sliced celery
- ½ tsp. salt
- ¼ tsp. pepper
- 1   can (10¾ oz.) condensed cream of celery soup, undiluted
- 3   cups frozen Tater Tots
- 1   cup shredded cheddar cheese

    Chopped fresh parsley or chives, optional

EQUIPMENT

- Large skillet
- Knife & cutting board
- Measuring cups & spoons
- Kitchen spoon
- 3-qt. baking dish

1. Preheat oven to 400°. In a large skillet, cook beef, onion and celery until meat is no longer pink and vegetables are tender; drain. Stir in salt and pepper.

2. Spoon mixture into a greased 3-qt. baking dish. Spread with soup. Top with frozen Tater Tots. Bake for 40 minutes or until bubbly. Sprinkle with cheese. Bake for 5 minutes or until cheese is melted. If desired, top with parsley or chives.

1 CUP 353 cal., 20g fat (8g sat. fat), 59mg chol., 1040mg sod., 25g carb. (2g sugars, 3g fiber), 21g pro.

How to Chop Herbs Fast

The wheel of a pizza cutter spins and cuts in both directions, making it ideal for chopping herbs. Simply bunch up the herbs and run the pizza cutter back and forth until they're chopped as finely as desired. Keep your fingers free of the wheel.

SKILL LEVEL 3

INGREDIENTS

- 1 **roasting chicken (5 to 6 lbs.)**
- ½ **cup unsalted butter, softened, divided**
- 1 **cup chicken broth**
- ¾ **cup orange juice**
- 2 **garlic cloves, minced**
- 1 **tsp. salt**
- ½ **tsp. pepper**
- 2 **fresh rosemary sprigs**
- 2 **fresh thyme sprigs**
- 2 **fresh sage sprigs**

EQUIPMENT

- **Toothpicks**
- **Roasting pan with rack**
- **Kitchen twine**
- **Measuring cups & spoons**
- **Brush**
- **Small bowl**
- **Thermometer**

Buttery Herb Roasted Chicken

Roasting chicken is always such a comforting thing, especially when you can pick the herbs right from your garden and pair them with some fresh citrus to smear across the bird! My family can't get enough of this herb-roasted chicken recipe.

—Jenn Tidwell, Fair Oaks, CA

PREP: 15 min. • **BAKE:** 1½ hours + standing • **MAKES:** 6 servings

1. Preheat oven to 350°. With fingers, carefully loosen skin from chicken; rub ¼ cup butter under skin. Secure skin to underside of breast with toothpicks. Place chicken on a rack in a shallow roasting pan, breast side up. Tuck wings under chicken; tie drumsticks together. Pour broth around chicken.

2. Melt remaining ¼ cup butter; brush over chicken. Drizzle with orange juice. In a small bowl, combine garlic, salt and pepper; rub over skin. Place rosemary, thyme and sage in roasting pan.

3. Roast for 1½-2 hours or until a thermometer inserted into thickest part of thigh reads 170°-175°. (Cover loosely with foil if chicken browns too quickly.) Remove chicken from oven; tent with foil. Let stand 15 minutes before carving; remove toothpicks. If desired, skim fat and thicken pan drippings for gravy. Serve with chicken.

6 OZ. COOKED CHICKEN 599 cal., 42g fat (17g sat. fat), 191mg chol., 703mg sod., 4g carb. (3g sugars, 0 fiber), 48g pro.

> *"I like to help my mom and dad make roast chicken. I spread butter all over it to make the skin crispy. I have to wash my hands a lot when I make it."*
> —ROWAN C., AGE 9

How to Truss a Chicken

Bend the wings at their elbow joints and tuck wings under the chicken. Use kitchen twine or unwaxed dental floss to tie the ankles tightly together, close to the body. Your goal is to make a tight, compact shape. This looks attractive and helps the chicken cook evenly.

Adam S., age 4, turns his hot dog into a race-car driver with help from his mom, Jenni. His car has pickle wheels, cherry tomato lights and a pretzel steering wheel. Give the driver a mustard face and olive helmet, and you'll be ready to roll.

SKILL LEVEL
1

INGREDIENTS

1 pkg. (1 lb.) hot dogs

2 cans (15 oz. each) chili without beans

1 can (10¾ oz.) condensed cheddar cheese soup, undiluted

1 can (4 oz.) chopped green chiles

10 hot dog buns, split

1 medium onion, chopped

1 to 2 cups corn chips, coarsely crushed

1 cup shredded cheddar cheese

EQUIPMENT

- 3-qt. slow cooker
- Large bowl
- Kitchen spoon
- Knife & cutting board

Bandito Chili Dogs from the Slow Cooker

These deluxe chili dogs are a surefire hit at all my family functions. Adults and children alike love the cheesy chili sauce, and the toppings are so fun!
—Marion Lowery, Medford, OR

PREP: 15 min. • **COOK:** 4 hours • **MAKES:** 10 servings

1. Place hot dogs in a 3-qt. slow cooker. In a large bowl, combine chili, soup and green chiles; pour over hot dogs. Cover and cook on low for 4-5 hours.

2. Serve hot dogs in buns; top with chili mixture, onion, corn chips and cheese.

1 CHILI DOG 450 cal., 23g fat (10g sat. fat), 53mg chol., 1442mg sod., 43g carb. (6g sugars, 3g fiber), 19g pro.

"These taste just like the coneys you get from Sonic, and they are so easy to prepare. One of our favorite meals."
—MMAHALA, TASTEOFHOME.COM

INGREDIENTS

- 1 pkg. (16 oz.) baby carrots
- 1 Tbsp. water
- 2 Tbsp. butter
- 2 Tbsp. honey
- 1 Tbsp. lemon juice

EQUIPMENT

- 1½-qt. microwave-safe dish
- Measuring spoon
- Microwave
- Large skillet
- Kitchen spoon

Honey-Glazed Carrots

My mother used sugar in this recipe, but a local man who keeps bees on our farm shares honey with us so I use that instead.

—Judie Anglen, Riverton, WY

TAKES: 10 min. • **MAKES:** 4 servings

1. Place carrots and water in a 1½-qt. microwave-safe dish. Cover and microwave until crisp-tender, 3-5 minutes.

2. Meanwhile, melt butter in a large skillet over low heat; stir in honey and lemon juice. Cook, stirring constantly, 3-4 minutes. Add carrots; cook and stir until glazed, about 1 minute.

½ CUP 124 cal., 6g fat (4g sat. fat), 15mg chol., 126mg sod., 20g carb. (14g sugars, 3g fiber), 1g pro.

> **"I like finding new ways to use vegetables to make good-tasting food."**
> —KATIE H., AGE 8

SKILL LEVEL 2

INGREDIENTS

1 pkg. (20 oz.) refrigerated cheese ravioli

3½ cups pasta sauce

2 cups small-curd 4% cottage cheese

4 cups shredded mozzarella cheese

¼ cup grated Parmesan cheese

Minced fresh parsley, optional

EQUIPMENT

- **Large pot for boiling ravioli**
- **Kitchen spoon**
- **Strainer for cooked ravioli**
- **Measuring cups**
- **13x9-in. baking dish**

Ravioli Casserole

The whole family will love this yummy dish that tastes like lasagna without all the fuss. Time-saving ingredients like prepared spaghetti sauce and frozen ravioli make it a cinch to put together. Children can help you assemble this one.

—**Mary Ann Rothert, Austin, TX**

PREP: 10 min. • **BAKE:** 30 min. • **MAKES:** 8 servings

1. Preheat oven to 350°. Prepare ravioli according to package directions; drain. Spread 1 cup pasta sauce in an ungreased 13x9-in. baking dish. Layer with half the ravioli, 1¼ cups sauce, 1 cup cottage cheese and 2 cups mozzarella cheese. Repeat layers. Sprinkle with Parmesan cheese.

2. Bake, uncovered, until bubbly, 30-40 minutes. Let stand for 5-10 minutes before serving. If desired, sprinkle with parsley.

1 CUP 518 cal., 25g fat (12g sat. fat), 88mg chol., 1411mg sod., 44g carb. (13g sugars, 5g fiber), 30g pro.

Make It Your Own!

For a meaty version, use meat-filled ravioli instead of cheese ones. Or add a layer of sliced cooked Italian sausages or frozen fully cooked meatballs. (Increase the cook time if you add frozen meat.)

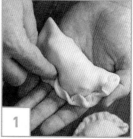

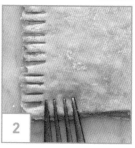

How to Seal Pizza Pockets (2 Ways)

#1 ROPED EDGE

Start at one end of the pocket. Pinch a small bit of dough between your forefinger and thumb. Gently stretch the dough away from the pizza pocket, then press it down on top of pocket to seal. Continue, making a pattern that chefs call a roped edge.

#2 CRIMPED EDGE

Fold the dough into pockets and press the edges shut with a fork. This way is easy. Try some of each!

SKILL LEVEL 3

Pepperoni Pizza Pockets

Stuffed with a pizza-style filling, these special sandwiches surprise you with a burst of flavor in every bite. They were popular at our son's birthday party, but you can be sure adults will love them too!

—Robin Werner, Brush Prairie, WA

PREP: 1 hour • **BAKE:** 20 min. • **MAKES:** 16 pockets

INGREDIENTS

- 2 pkg. (¼ oz. each) active dry yeast
- 2 cups warm water (110° to 115°)
- 2 Tbsp. sugar
- 2 Tbsp. butter, melted
- 2 tsp. salt
- 6 to 6½ cups all-purpose flour
- 1 can (8 oz.) pizza sauce, divided
- 96 slices turkey pepperoni
- 4 cups shredded part-skim mozzarella cheese
- 1 large egg, lightly beaten
- 8 tsp. grated Parmesan cheese
- 2 tsp. Italian seasoning

EQUIPMENT

- Large bowl
- Measuring cups & spoons
- Kitchen spoon
- Rolling pin
- Pastry brush
- Baking sheets

1. Preheat oven to 400°. In a large bowl, dissolve yeast in warm water. Add sugar, butter, salt and 4½ cups flour. Beat until smooth. Stir in enough remaining flour to form a soft dough.

2. Turn onto a floured surface; knead until smooth and elastic, 6-8 minutes. Divide dough into 16 pieces. On a lightly floured surface, roll each dough portion into a 6-in. circle. Place 2 tsp. pizza sauce, 6 slices pepperoni and ¼ cup mozzarella on each circle. Lightly brush edge of dough with beaten egg. Bring dough over filling; press firmly, then crimp seams to seal.

3. Place on greased or parchment-lined baking sheets. Brush with egg; sprinkle with Parmesan cheese and Italian seasoning. Bake until golden brown, 18-20 minutes. Warm remaining pizza sauce; serve with pizza pockets.

1 POCKET 316 cal., 9g fat (5g sat. fat), 47mg chol., 751mg sod., 41g carb. (3g sugars, 2g fiber), 16g pro.

"I am 8 years old. I chose this recipe for my turn to cook on family night. My whole family loved it so much they couldn't stop eating. This was the first thing I have ever cooked that was homemade."

—FRIDAYNIGHTCHILI, TASTEOFHOME.COM

SKILL LEVEL 2

Tacos Deluxe

I first tried this recipe in my junior high school home economics class some 20 years ago. As an adult, I wrote home for the recipe and have enjoyed it ever since!
—Katie Dreibelbis, Santa Clara, CA

PREP: 25 min. • **BAKE:** 10 min. • **MAKES:** 8 servings

1. In a large skillet, cook beef and onion over medium heat, breaking beef into crumbles, until meat is no longer pink; drain. Add the next 12 ingredients to meat mixture. Simmer, uncovered, until liquid is almost completely reduced, stirring occasionally, 10-15 minutes. Cool slightly; stir in cheese.

2. Preheat oven to 400°. Place taco shells open end up in a baking pan; place 1 scoop meat mixture into each shell. Bake until meat is hot and cheese is melted, 10-15 minutes.

3. Sprinkle lettuce and tomatoes over tacos. In a small bowl, combine dressing ingredients; drizzle over tacos. If desired, top with jalapeno and red onion.

1 TACO 312 cal., 19g fat (6g sat. fat), 44mg chol., 874mg sod., 21g carb. (12g sugars, 1g fiber), 13g pro.

INGREDIENTS

- 1 lb. ground beef
- 2 Tbsp. chopped onion
- 1 can (15 oz.) tomato sauce
- 1 tsp. white vinegar
- 1 tsp. Worcestershire sauce
- 2 to 3 drops hot pepper sauce
- 1 tsp. sugar
- 1 tsp. chili powder
- ½ tsp. garlic salt
- ¼ tsp. celery salt
- ¼ tsp. onion salt
- ⅛ tsp. ground allspice
- ⅛ tsp. ground cinnamon
  Dash pepper
- ½ cup shredded cheddar cheese
- 8 taco shells
  Shredded lettuce
  Chopped tomatoes

SWEET-AND-SOUR DRESSING

- 1 cup Miracle Whip
- ⅓ cup sugar
- 2 Tbsp. white vinegar
- ¼ tsp. salt
- ½ tsp. hot pepper sauce
  Optional: Sliced jalapeno pepper and red onion

Make It Your Own!

Omit the dressing and serve the tacos with salsa, picante sauce or a sweet bottled dressing you like from the fridge. Catalina or Western dressing would be delicious here. Add your favorite taco toppings.

EQUIPMENT

- Large skillet
- Knife & cutting board
- Measuring cups & spoons
- Kitchen spoons
- Strainer for cooked meat
- Baking pan
- Small bowl

SKILL LEVEL 2

INGREDIENTS

- 1 lb. ground beef
- 2 tsp. Montreal steak seasoning
- 6 cups torn iceberg lettuce
- 2 cups shredded cheddar cheese
- 1 cup salad croutons
- 1 medium tomato, chopped
- 1 small onion, halved and thinly sliced
- ½ cup dill pickle slices
- Thousand Island salad dressing

EQUIPMENT

- Bowls
- Measuring cups & spoon
- Trays for uncooked and cooked patties
- Grill
- Turner
- Thermometer

ADULT HELP

Cheeseburger Salad

I was planning to grill burgers, then I decided to make a cheeseburger salad instead. The taste will remind you of a McDonalds Big Mac. You can add other favorite burger toppings, like crumbled cooked bacon, or even hot onion rings or french fries.
—**Pam Jefferies, Cantrall, IL**

TAKES: 30 min. • **MAKES:** 4 servings

1. In a large bowl, combine beef and steak seasoning, mixing lightly but thoroughly. Shape into twenty ½-in.-thick patties. Grill mini burgers, covered, over medium heat, 3-4 minutes on each side or until a thermometer reads 160°.

2. In another large bowl, combine lettuce, mini burgers, cheese, croutons, tomato, onion and pickles. Serve with salad dressing.

FREEZE OPTION Place patties on a waxed paper-lined baking sheet; cover and freeze until firm. Remove from sheet and transfer to an airtight container; return to freezer. To use, cook frozen patties as directed, increasing time as necessary for a thermometer to read 160°.

1 SERVING 511 cal., 34g fat (17g sat. fat), 128mg chol., 1033mg sod., 14g carb. (4g sugars, 3g fiber), 36g pro.

The Game Plan

LITTLE KIDS CAN …
Gather the equipment, shape the patties and get the door for the adult who's grilling the patties.

BIG KIDS CAN …
Prepare the salad ingredients and help the adult who's grilling the patties.

SKILL LEVEL 2

INGREDIENTS

- 1 can (15 oz.) tomato sauce
- 1 can (6 oz.) tomato paste
- 1 tsp. dried basil
- ½ tsp. garlic salt
- ¼ tsp. onion powder
- ¼ tsp. sugar
- 1 tube (11 oz.) refrigerated thin pizza crust
- 1½ cups shredded part-skim mozzarella cheese

OPTIONAL TOPPINGS

Pepperoni, olives, sausage, onion, green pepper, Canadian bacon, pineapple, tomatoes, fresh basil and crushed red pepper flakes

EQUIPMENT

- Small bowl
- Measuring cups & spoons
- Knife & cutting board
- Muffin tins

Mini Pizza Cups

I just baked these mini pizzas, and the kids are already asking for more. The no-cook pizza sauce and refrigerated dough make this meal a snap.

—Melissa Haines, Valparaiso, IN

PREP: 25 min. • **BAKE:** 10 min. • **MAKES:** 8 servings

1. Preheat oven to 425°. In a small bowl, mix first 6 ingredients.

2. Unroll pizza dough; cut into 16 squares. Press squares onto bottoms and up sides of 16 ungreased muffin cups, allowing corners to hang over edges.

3. Spoon 1 Tbsp. sauce mixture into each cup. Top with cheese; add optional toppings as desired. Bake for 10-12 minutes or until crust is golden brown. Serve pizzas with the remaining sauce mixture.

FREEZE OPTION Freeze cooled baked pizzas in a resealable freezer container. To use, reheat pizzas on a baking sheet in a preheated 425° oven until heated through.

2 PIZZAS WITH 2 TBSP. SAUCE 209 cal., 8g fat (3g sat. fat), 14mg chol., 747mg sod., 26g carb. (5g sugars, 2g fiber), 10g pro.

Looking Good.

Here's a nice chance to make each family member's favorite, so get creative and mix up the different toppings. Add fresh and colorful ingredients at the very end of baking to preserve their colors. Think about sliced basil leaves or red and golden pear tomatoes, cut in half.

INGREDIENTS

- **8 cups fresh green beans, trimmed**
- **4 bacon strips, chopped**
- **½ cup chopped onion**
- **¼ tsp. salt**
- **⅛ tsp. pepper**

EQUIPMENT

- **Measuring cups & spoons**
- **Large saucepan**
- **Strainer for cooked beans**
- **Knife & cutting board**
- **Large skillet**
- **Kitchen spoon**

Green Beans with Bacon

Bits of bacon and onion dress up the green beans in this easy-to-prepare side dish. These beans lend a crisp, fresh flavor to any meal from steaks to chicken.

—**Mari Anne Warren, Milton, WI**

TAKES: 25 min. • **MAKES:** 8 servings

1. Place beans in a large saucepan and cover with water. Bring to a boil. Cook, uncovered, 8-10 minutes or until beans are crisp-tender; drain. In a large skillet, cook bacon and onion over medium heat until bacon is crisp and onion is tender, stirring occasionally, 3-5 minutes.

2. Add beans to bacon mixture. Sprinkle with salt and pepper; toss to coat.

1 CUP 62 cal., 2g fat (1g sat. fat), 6mg chol., 177mg sod., 8g carb. (4g sugars, 3g fiber), 4g pro. **DIABETIC EXCHANGES** 1 vegetable, ½ fat.

How to Trim Green Beans

Before you get cooking, remove the tough, withered ends from the beans. You can pinch them off with your fingers or use kitchen shears.

INGREDIENTS

- 12 oz. uncooked spaghetti
- 1 lb. ground beef
- 1 envelope taco seasoning
- ¾ cup water
- 1 can (15 oz.) black beans, rinsed and drained
- 1 can (10 oz.) diced tomatoes and green chiles, undrained
- 2 cups shredded Mexican cheese blend, divided
- ⅔ cup salsa

EQUIPMENT

- Large pot for boiling spaghetti
- Dutch oven
- Kitchen spoon
- Measuring cups
- Strainers for cooked spaghetti & meat
- 13x9-in. baking dish

Taco Spaghetti

I came up with this kid-friendly southwestern recipe one afternoon when I was using up leftover spaghetti and ground beef. When I'm lucky enough to have extra time, I make two batches and freeze one.

—J. Vanness, Wichita, KS

PREP: 20 min. • **BAKE:** 25 min. • **MAKES:** 8 servings

1. Preheat oven to 350°. Break spaghetti into thirds; cook according to package directions for al dente.

2. Meanwhile, in a Dutch oven, cook beef over medium heat 6-8 minutes or until no longer pink, breaking into crumbles; drain. Stir in taco seasoning and water; bring to a boil. Reduce heat; simmer, uncovered, 5 minutes, stirring occasionally.

3. Stir in beans, tomatoes, 1 cup cheese and salsa. Drain spaghetti; add to beef mixture and toss to combine.

4. Transfer to a greased 13x9-in. baking dish. Bake, covered, 20 minutes. Sprinkle with remaining cheese. Bake, uncovered, 3-5 minutes longer or until cheese is melted. Let stand for 5 minutes before serving.

FREEZE OPTION Cool unbaked casserole; sprinkle with remaining cheese. Cover and freeze. To use, partially thaw in refrigerator overnight. Remove from refrigerator 30 minutes before baking. Preheat oven to 350°. Bake casserole, covered, 55-60 minutes or until hot and a thermometer inserted in center reads 165°.

1 SERVING 439 cal., 16g fat (7g sat. fat), 60mg chol., 927mg sod., 47g carb. (2g sugars, 4g fiber), 24g pro.

Did You Know?

Italians like to eat their spaghetti with a fork *and* spoon. They get a forkful of spaghetti, then place the ends of the fork against a soup spoon they're holding in their other hand. Then they twist, twist away until the spaghetti coils up into a bundle on their fork, making it easy to pop into the mouth. The twirling spaghetti looks like it's dancing!

Chicken Nuggets

I like to make these golden chicken nuggets because they're so quick and easy. The whole family loves them. The seasoning can also be used on chicken breast halves to make amazing sandwiches.

—Annette Ellyson, Carolina, WV

INGREDIENTS

- 1 cup all-purpose flour
- 4 tsp. seasoned salt
- 1 tsp. poultry seasoning
- 1 tsp. ground mustard
- 1 tsp. paprika
- ½ tsp. pepper
- 2 lbs. boneless skinless chicken breasts
- ¼ cup canola oil

TAKES: 30 min. • **MAKES:** 8 servings

1. In a large shallow dish, combine first 6 ingredients. Flatten chicken to ½-in. thickness, then cut into 1½-in. pieces. Add chicken, a few pieces at a time, to dish and turn to coat.

2. In a large skillet, cook chicken in oil in batches, turning once using tongs, until meat is no longer pink, 6-8 minutes.

3 OZ. COOKED CHICKEN 214 cal., 10g fat (1g sat. fat), 63mg chol., 435mg sod., 6g carb. (0 sugars, 0 fiber), 24g pro. **DIABETIC EXCHANGES** 3 lean meat, 1½ fat, ½ starch.

How to Flatten Chicken Breasts

Place boneless chicken breasts between two pieces of waxed paper or kitchen wrap. Starting in the center and working out to the edges, pound lightly with a meat mallet until the chicken is an even thickness. No meat mallet? Use a small pan, a can of vegetables or even a clean hammer.

"Chicken nuggets are life."

—MACI G., AGE 10

EQUIPMENT

- Large shallow dish
- Measuring cups & spoons
- Kitchen spoon
- Meat mallet
- Knife & cutting board
- Large skillet
- Tongs

INGREDIENTS

- **6** boneless pork loin chops (6 oz. each)
- **1** Tbsp. canola oil
- **1** pkg. (6 oz.) crushed stuffing mix
- **1** can (21 oz.) apple pie filling with cinnamon

  Minced fresh parsley, optional

EQUIPMENT

- **Large skillet**
- **Measuring cup & spoon**
- **Tongs**
- **Saucepan with lid**
- **Kitchen spoon**
- **13x9-in. baking dish**
- **Thermometer**

Pork Chops with Apples & Stuffing

Heartwarming cinnamon and apples are the perfect accompaniment to these tender pork chops. The dish is always a winner with my family. Because it calls for only four ingredients, it's an easy main dish to make with little prep time.

—Joan Hamilton, Worcester, MA

PREP: 15 min. • **BAKE:** 45 min. • **MAKES:** 6 servings

1. In a large skillet, brown pork chops in oil over medium-high heat, using tongs to turn chops. Meanwhile, prepare stuffing according to package directions. Spread pie filling into a greased 13x9-in. baking dish. Place chops on top; spoon stuffing over the pork chops.

2. Cover and bake at 350° for 35 minutes. Uncover; bake until a thermometer inserted in pork reads 145°, about 10 minutes longer. If desired, sprinkle with parsley.

1 SERVING 527 cal., 21g fat (9g sat. fat), 102mg chol., 550mg sod., 48g carb. (15g sugars, 3g fiber), 36g pro.

How to Prep Parsley Fast

To remove parsley leaves quickly and easily, run a fork along the stem. This will gently remove the leaves. Mince with a chef's knife or leave as is for a more rustic look.

SKILL LEVEL 1

INGREDIENTS

- 1 carton (15 oz.) part-skim ricotta cheese
- 1 pkg. (10 oz.) frozen chopped spinach, thawed and squeezed dry
- 2½ cups shredded Italian cheese blend
- ½ cup diced red onion
- ½ tsp. garlic powder
- 2 tsp. dried basil
- ½ tsp. dried oregano
- ½ tsp. dried thyme
- 2 jars (24 oz. each) roasted garlic Parmesan pasta sauce
- 2 cups water
- 1 pkg. (12 oz.) jumbo pasta shells

  Optional: Additional shredded Italian cheese blend and sliced fresh basil

EQUIPMENT

- Bowl
- Measuring cups & spoons
- Kitchen spoon
- 6-qt. slow cooker
- Spoon or piping bag

Slow-Cooker Stuffed Shells

There's no need to precook the shells in this simple pasta dish. It's almost like magic to lift the lid and find such deliciousness ready to serve. Add garlic bread and you're golden!
—Sherry Day, Pinckney, MI

PREP: 30 min. • **COOK:** 4 hours • **MAKES:** 10 servings

1. In a bowl, mix the first 8 ingredients (mixture will be stiff). In a greased 6-qt. slow cooker, mix 1 jar pasta sauce with water. Using a spoon or piping bag, fill pasta shells with ricotta mixture; layer in slow cooker. Top with remaining jar of pasta sauce.

2. Cook, covered, on low until pasta is tender, 4-5 hours. Serve with additional cheese and fresh basil as desired.

4 STUFFED SHELLS 303 cal., 10g fat (6g sat. fat), 34mg chol., 377mg sod., 34g carb. (4g sugars, 3g fiber), 17g pro. **DIABETIC EXCHANGES** 2 starch, 2 medium-fat meat.

"I love this recipe. I leave out the spinach because my husband won't touch anything with spinach. It still tastes wonderful! The uncooked shells are pretty easy to stuff, too, especially if you let the ricotta come to room temperature first.
—KINCSEM, TASTEOFHOME.COM

Gerardo S., age 9, loves his burgers with a side of french fries dipped in ice cream!

Cheeseburger Cups

A terrific recipe for busy families, this simple, inexpensive dish is made with handy ingredients and takes just a short time. Best of all, kids go crazy for these darling dinner bites!

—Jeri Millhouse, Ashland, OH

TAKES: 30 min. • **MAKES:** 10 servings

INGREDIENTS

- 1 lb. ground beef
- ½ cup ketchup
- 2 Tbsp. brown sugar
- 1 Tbsp. prepared mustard
- 1½ tsp. Worcestershire sauce
- 2 tubes (10½ oz. each) large refrigerated buttermilk biscuits
- ½ cup cubed Velveeta

EQUIPMENT

- Large skillet
- Kitchen spoon
- Strainer for cooked meat
- Measuring cup & spoons
- Muffin tin
- Knife & cutting board

1. In a large skillet, cook beef over medium heat until no longer pink, breaking it into crumbles; drain. Stir in ketchup, brown sugar, mustard and Worcestershire sauce. Remove from heat; set aside.

2. Press each biscuit onto bottom and up side of a greased muffin cup. Spoon beef mixture into cups; top with cheese cubes. Bake at 400° until cups are golden brown, 14-16 minutes.

1 CHEESEBURGER CUP 299 cal., 14g fat (5g sat. fat), 34mg chol., 910mg sod., 32g carb. (9g sugars, 1g fiber), 13g pro.

Mushroom & Swiss Burger Cups Add 1 cup chopped mushrooms to the beef as it browns, and cook until softened. Then, swap the cubed Swiss cheese in for the Velveeta.

Bacon Cheeseburger Cups Add ½ cup cooked and crumbled bacon to the beef filling.

Taco Burger Cups Omit brown sugar, mustard and Worcestershire sauce from the filling. Swap in a packet of taco seasoning mix instead. Serve the burger cups with your favorite taco toppings.

Turkey Cheeseburger Cups Replace the ground beef with 1 lb. ground turkey.

Vegetarian Cheeseburger Cups Swap out the ground beef for a pound of crumbly plant-based meat substitute. Omit the Worcestershire sauce, as it probably contains fish.

SKILL LEVEL
2

INGREDIENTS

- 1 lb. ground beef
- 1 large onion, chopped
- 2 garlic cloves, minced
- 1 can (29 oz.) tomato sauce
- 1 cup water
- 1 can (6 oz.) tomato paste
- 1 tsp. salt
- 1 tsp. dried oregano
- 1 pkg. (8 oz.) no-cook lasagna noodles
- 4 cups shredded part-skim mozzarella cheese
- 1½ cups 4% cottage cheese
- ½ cup grated Parmesan cheese

EQUIPMENT

- Large skillet
- Knife & cutting board
- Kitchen spoon
- Strainer for cooked meat
- Measuring cups & spoons
- 5-qt. slow cooker
- Large bowl

Slow-Cooker Lasagna

No-cook lasagna noodles make this traditional favorite easy to prepare in the slow cooker. Because it's so simple to make, it's great to whip up on any day. We like it with Parmesan bread or garlic cheese toast.

—Lisa Micheletti, Collierville, TN

PREP: 25 min. • **COOK:** 4 hours • **MAKES:** 8 servings

1. In a large skillet, cook beef and onion over medium heat until meat is no longer pink. Add garlic; cook 1 minute longer. Drain. Stir in tomato sauce, water, tomato paste, salt and oregano.

2. Spread a fourth of the meat sauce in an ungreased 5-qt. slow cooker. Arrange a third of the noodles over sauce (break noodles to fit if necessary). Combine cheeses in a large bowl; spoon a third of the mixture over noodles. Repeat layers twice. Top with remaining meat sauce.

3. Cover and cook on low for 4-5 hours or until noodles are tender.

1 PIECE 510 cal., 23g fat (11g sat. fat), 89mg chol., 1464mg sod., 39g carb. (9g sugars, 4g fiber), 38g pro.

★★★★★

"Wonderful! I had a bit left over, and my son actually had it for breakfast the next morning. I will definitely make this again ... a lot!"

—KAT83, TASTEOFHOME.COM

PAGE 151

SNACKS & DRINKS

SKILL LEVEL 2

Hot Dog Sliders

We wanted to get creative with hot dogs, so we made a mac-and-cheesy one. Pile yours with extra cheese, canned chili or even bacon.
—Julie Peterson, Crofton, MD

PREP: 25 min. + rising • **BAKE:** 15 min. + cooling • **MAKES:** 2 dozen

1. Let dough stand at room temperature until soft enough to shape, 15-20 minutes. Cut each roll in half; shape each half into a 3-in.-long mini hot dog bun. Place 2 in. apart on greased baking sheets.

2. Cover with greased plastic wrap; let rise in a warm place until almost doubled, about 45 minutes. Preheat oven to 350°.

3. Bake buns until golden brown, 12-15 minutes. Remove from pans to wire racks to cool completely.

4. In a 15x10x1-in. baking pan, toss bread crumbs with onion, oil, salt and pepper. Bake at 350° until golden brown, stirring once, 5-7 minutes.

5. Cook hot dogs and macaroni and cheese according to package directions. To serve, cut hot dogs crosswise in half. Split buns; fill with hot dogs and macaroni and cheese. Sprinkle with toasted crumbs.

1 APPETIZER 198 cal., 12g fat (5g sat. fat), 25mg chol., 446mg sod., 18g carb. (2g sugars, 1g fiber), 6g pro.

"These were fun to put together with my son."
—ANGEL182009, TASTEOFHOME.COM

INGREDIENTS

- 1 pkg. (16 oz.) frozen bread dough dinner rolls (12 count), thawed but still cold
- ½ cup panko bread crumbs
- 2 Tbsp. chopped onion
- 1 Tbsp. canola oil
- ¼ tsp. salt
- ⅛ tsp. pepper
- 12 bun-length beef hot dogs
- 1 pkg. (7¼ oz.) macaroni and cheese dinner mix

EQUIPMENT

- Knife & cutting board
- Baking sheets
- Wire racks
- 15x10x1-in. baking pan
- Measuring cup & spoons
- Saucepans, tongs, kitchen spoon & strainer for cooking hot dogs & macaroni

"For Ellie's third birthday, she only wanted mac & cheese. I painstakingly made her a homemade mac & cheese, to which she said: 'No. I mean REAL mac & cheese, the kind from the blue box.'"

—ANDREA K., MOM

Gross Garnish Idea

Loop a gummy worm around the rim and handle of each punch cup. If your cups don't have handles, cut a notch in the worm with a small knife or kitchen shears. Then stick the notch onto the rim of the cup.

SKILL LEVEL 1

INGREDIENTS

1 can (12 oz.) frozen orange juice concentrate, thawed

2 liters lemon-lime soda, chilled

1 can (46 oz.) pineapple juice, chilled

1 qt. orange or pineapple sherbet

EQUIPMENT

- Pitcher & kitchen spoon
- Punch bowl
- Ice cream scoop

Orange Party Punch

This citrus punch was served at every birthday party I had when I was growing up. Now I prepare it for my kids. You can float orange slices between the scoops of sherbet for extra flair.

—Brenda Rupert, Clyde, OH

TAKES: 10 min. • **MAKES:** 5½ qt.

Prepare orange juice according to package directions; pour into a punch bowl. Stir in soda and pineapple juice. Top with scoops of sherbet. Serve immediately.

1 CUP 142 cal., 1g fat (0 sat. fat), 2mg chol., 24mg sod., 34g carb. (32g sugars, 0 fiber), 1g pro.

Make It Your Own!

USE DIFFERENT JUICES. For a super-summery version, use frozen lemonade concentrate instead of orange juice, and mango or passion fruit juice instead of pineapple.

PLAY WITH THE SHERBET FLAVORS. Try other flavor combinations like lemon, lime, strawberry and more.

TOP WITH VANILLA ICE CREAM. Want to make a drinkable orange creamsicle? Use vanilla ice cream instead of sherbet.

Frozen Banana Cereal Pops

When we want a healthy snack, we dip bananas in yogurt, roll 'em in cereal, then freeze. Ta-da!
—Scarlett Elrod, Newnan, GA

INGREDIENTS

- ¾ cup strawberry yogurt
- 2 cups Fruity Pebbles cereal
- 4 medium bananas, peeled and cut crosswise in half
- 8 wooden pop sticks

EQUIPMENT

- Shallow bowls
- Measuring cups
- Knife & cutting board
- Pop sticks
- Baking sheet

PREP: 15 min. + freezing • **MAKES:** 8 pops

1. Place yogurt and cereal in separate shallow bowls. Insert pop sticks through cut side of bananas. Dip bananas in yogurt, then roll in cereal to coat. Transfer to a waxed paper-lined baking sheet.

2. Freeze until firm, about 1 hour. Transfer to an airtight freezer container; seal container and return pops to freezer.

1 POP 106 cal., 1g fat (1g sat. fat), 1mg chol., 57mg sod., 24g carb. (14g sugars, 2g fiber), 2g pro. **DIABETIC EXCHANGES** 1 starch, ½ fruit.

Make It Your Own!

Switch it up with vanilla yogurt and Cocoa Pebbles cereal.

SKILL LEVEL 1

Slow-Cooked Beefy Nachos

Nachos you can feel good about! This meaty topping has less fat and sodium than typical nacho beef because you use lean meat and make your own seasoning. The versatile dish is great for a party.
—Carol Betz, Grand Rapids, MI

PREP: 15 min. • **COOK:** 4 hours • **MAKES:** 20 servings (2½ qt.)

INGREDIENTS

- 2 **lbs. lean ground beef (90% lean)**
- 1 **can (15 oz.) Ranch Style beans (pinto beans in seasoned tomato sauce), undrained**
- 2 **Tbsp. chili powder**
- 1 **Tbsp. brown sugar**
- 2 **tsp. ground cumin**
- 2 **tsp. ground coriander**
- 1 **tsp. dried oregano**
- 1 **tsp. cayenne pepper**
- 1 **Tbsp. cider vinegar**
- ¾ **tsp. salt**

  Baked tortilla chips

  Optional: Shredded cheddar cheese, lettuce, sour cream and guacamole

EQUIPMENT

- 4-qt. slow cooker
- Measuring spoons
- Kitchen spoon

Combine first 8 ingredients in a 4-qt. slow cooker. Cook, covered, on low until meat is no longer pink, 4-6 hours. Stir in vinegar and salt, breaking meat into crumbles. Serve with tortilla chips and, if desired, toppings.

FREEZE OPTION Freeze cooled meat mixture in freezer containers. To use, partially thaw in refrigerator overnight. Heat through in a saucepan, stirring occasionally. Add water if necessary. Serve with chips and toppings if desired.

½ CUP 99 cal., 4g fat (2g sat. fat), 28mg chol., 232mg sod., 5g carb. (1g sugars, 1g fiber), 10g pro.

> **"I love that it has a lot of cheese and chips. And when you heat it up, it's actually really good."**
> **—ELIAS F., AGE 6**

SKILL LEVEL 1

INGREDIENTS

2 **cups frozen pineapple chunks**

1 **cup vanilla ice cream**

½ **cup unsweetened pineapple juice**

EQUIPMENT

- **Blender**
- **Measuring cups**
- **Spatula**
- **Piping bag & pastry tip**

Disney's Dole Whip

Your kitchen will be the happiest place on earth when you serve this sweet-sour treat. The recipe comes directly from the Disneyland app and tastes just like the real deal you'd order at the park.

—Taste of Home **Test Kitchen**

TAKES: 10 min. • **MAKES:** 2 servings

Place all ingredients in a blender; cover and process until thick, stopping and scraping side as needed. Pipe mixture into 2 bowls or glasses, topping each with a swirl.

1 CUP 290 cal., 7g fat (4g sat. fat), 29mg chol., 87mg sod., 50g carb. (34g sugars, 1g fiber), 3g pro.

Looking Good.

A piping bag with open star pastry tip (shown at lower right) gives this treat a fancy look. But you can skip this step and scoop the mixture right into bowls instead. Top each serving with whipped cream from a can to get the same look with no mess or need to have great piping skills. Then put a cherry on top of your frosty creations.

EQUIPMENT
- Measuring cups
- Knife & cutting board
- Kitchen spoon

Rainbow Spritzer

This drink gets its tangy, bubbly goodness from ginger ale and puckery lemonade.

—Olivia Thompson, Milwaukee, WI

INGREDIENTS

- ½ cup fresh blueberries
- ½ cup chopped peeled kiwifruit
- ½ cup chopped fresh pineapple
- ½ cup sliced fresh strawberries or fresh raspberries
- 1 cup chilled ginger ale
- ½ cup chilled unsweetened pineapple juice
- ½ cup chilled lemonade

TAKES: 20 min. • **MAKES:** 4 servings

In 4 tall glasses, layer blueberries, kiwi, pineapple and strawberries. In a 2-cup glass measure or small pitcher, mix remaining ingredients; pour over fruit. Serve immediately.

1 SERVING 91 cal., 0 fat (0 sat. fat), 0 chol., 8mg sod., 23g carb. (18g sugars, 2g fiber), 1g pro.

How to Peel a Kiwi (2 Ways)

#1 SLICE AND PEEL
Cut both ends from fruit. Using a vegetable peeler, peel off fuzzy brown peel.

#2 SCOOP WITH A SPOON
Cut both ends from fruit. Using a teaspoon, separate flesh from peel.

INGREDIENTS

1½ **cups white baking chips**

1 **pkg. (10 oz.) pretzel rods**

Colored candy stars or sprinkles

Colored sugar or edible glitter

EQUIPMENT

- Bowl
- Microwave
- Kitchen spoon

Magic Wands

These fun and colorful wands don't need to be made by a magician to be magical. You can change the colors to fit any party theme.

—Renee Schwebach, Dumont, MN

PREP: 25 min. + standing • **MAKES:** 2 dozen

In a microwave, melt chips; stir until smooth. Dip each pretzel rod halfway into melted chips; allow excess to drip off. Sprinkle coatings with candy stars and colored sugar. Place pretzels on waxed paper; let stand until dry. Store in an airtight container.

NOTE Edible glitter is available from Wilton Industries. Call 800-794-5866 or visit wilton.com.

1 WAND 103 cal., 4g fat (2g sat. fat), 2mg chol., 164mg sod., 15g carb. (0 sugars, 0 fiber), 2g pro.

Star-Spangled Berry Wands

Wash **strawberries**, **blueberries** and **watermelon**. Remove crowns from strawberries. Then, have an adult cut watermelon into 1-in.-thick slices. Cut melon with a star-shaped cutter. Then thread fruit onto skewers.

SKILL LEVEL 1

INGREDIENTS

- 1 pkg. (8 oz.) cream cheese, softened
- ¼ cup butter, softened
- 2 cups confectioners' sugar
- ⅓ cup baking cocoa
- ¼ cup 2% milk
- 2 Tbsp. brown sugar
- 1 tsp. vanilla extract

  Optional: M&M's minis and dark chocolate chips

  Graham crackers, pretzels and/or fresh strawberries

EQUIPMENT

- Large bowl
- Mixer or kitchen spoon
- Measuring cups & spoons

Brownie Batter Dip

I'm all about the sweeter side of dipsThis one tastes like brownie batter and fits my life's philosophy: Chocolate makes anything better. Grab some fruit, cookies or salty snacks and start dunking.

—Mel Gunnell, Boise, ID

TAKES: 10 min. • **MAKES:** 2½ cups

In a large bowl, beat cream cheese and butter until smooth. Beat in confectioners' sugar, cocoa, milk, brown sugar and vanilla until smooth. If desired, sprinkle with M&M's minis. Serve with dippers of your choice.

2 TBSP. 118 cal., 6g fat (4g sat. fat), 18mg chol., 56mg sod., 15g carb. (14g sugars, 0 fiber), 1g pro.

"Great dip! My favorite thing to dip in it? Strawberries, hands down. I think it tastes best if you let the flavors blend together for a few hours or overnight."

—ALLISONWILLIAMSON, TASTEOFHOME.COM

INGREDIENTS

- 2 **cups dry bread crumbs**
- 3 **Tbsp. all-purpose flour**
- 3 **large eggs**
- 2 **Tbsp. water**
- 1 **Tbsp. Italian seasoning**
- 1 **tsp. garlic powder**
- ¼ **tsp. pepper**
- 12 **sticks string cheese**
  Cooking spray
- 1 **cup marinara sauce or meatless pasta sauce, warmed**
  Chopped fresh basil, optional

EQUIPMENT

- **Small skillet**
- **Measuring cups & spoons**
- **Shallow bowls**
- **Fork**
- **Air fryer**

Air-Fryer Mozzarella Sticks

Deep-fried mozzarella sticks are one of our favorite appetizers. I figured out how to make them at home without having to haul out the deep fryer. Make sure to double-bread each one so the outsides get nice and crunchy, and to keep the cheese from oozing out as the sticks get warm.

—Mary Merchant, Barre, VT

PREP: 15 min. + freezing • **COOK:** 10 min. • **MAKES:** 1 dozen

1. In a small skillet, toast bread crumbs until lightly browned, about 1-2 minutes. Cool completely.

2. Place flour in a shallow bowl. In another shallow bowl, beat eggs and water with a fork. In a third shallow bowl, combine bread crumbs, Italian seasoning, garlic powder and pepper. Coat cheese sticks with flour, then dip into egg mixture and coat with bread crumb mixture. Repeat egg and bread crumb coatings. Cover and freeze cheese sticks for 8 hours or overnight.

3. Preheat air fryer to 400°. Place cheese in a single layer on a greased tray in air-fryer basket; spritz with cooking spray. Cook until golden brown and heated through, 6-8 minutes, turning halfway through cooking and spritzing with additional cooking spray. Allow to stand 3-5 minutes before serving. Serve with marinara for dipping. If desired, sprinkle with basil.

NOTE Cook times vary dramatically among different brands of air fryers. Refer to your air-fryer manual for general cook times and adjust if necessary.

1 PIECE 148 cal., 8g fat (4g sat. fat), 46mg chol., 384mg sod., 10g carb. (2g sugars, 1g fiber), 11g pro.

Baked Mozzarella Sticks Place cheese sticks on a parchment-lined baking sheet, spray with cooking spray, and bake at 400° for 6-8 minutes or until heated through. Allow to stand 3-5 minutes before serving.

"I love stretchy cheese."
—ISABELLE P., AGE 7

"Everything is better
with chocolate chips."

–STELLA R., AGE 7

SKILL LEVEL 1

Chocolate Chip Dip

Is there a kid around (or a kid at heart) who wouldn't gobble up this creamy dip for graham crackers? It beats dunking them in milk, hands down! You can also use apple wedges for dipping.

—Heather Koenig, Prairie du Chien, WI

TAKES: 15 min. • **MAKES:** 2 cups

INGREDIENTS

- 1 pkg. (8 oz.) cream cheese, softened
- ½ cup butter, softened
- ¾ cup confectioners' sugar
- 2 Tbsp. brown sugar
- 1 tsp. vanilla extract
- 1 cup miniature semisweet chocolate chips
- Graham cracker sticks

EQUIPMENT

- Small bowl
- Measuring cups & spoons
- Mixer or kitchen spoon

In a small bowl, beat cream cheese and butter until light and fluffy. Add the sugars and vanilla; beat until smooth. Stir in chocolate chips. Serve with graham cracker sticks.

2 TBSP. 181 cal., 14g fat (8g sat. fat), 30mg chol., 92mg sod., 15g carb. (14g sugars, 1g fiber), 1g pro.

Make It Your Own!

ADD STIR-INS. In addition to the mini chips, consider chopped pecans or pistachios, butterscotch chips, toffee bits or mini M&Ms.

BRIGHTEN WITH AN ACCENT FLAVOR. Add a small amount of orange zest for a bright, citrusy accent. If you love chocolate-covered cherries, try a drop or 2 of almond or cherry extract.

MIX UP YOUR DIPPERS. Serve animal crackers, sugar wafer cookies or sliced fruits on the side.

TURN IT INTO CANNOLI. Pipe the mixture into store-bought cannoli shells, then cover the ends with chopped pistachios, miniature chocolate chips or confectioners' sugar. Or make cannoli sandwich cookies using vanilla wafers and this dip as a filling. Roll the edges of your cookies in finely chopped pistachios or mini chips.

INGREDIENTS

- 1 **cup whole milk**
- 2 **cups vanilla ice cream**
- ½ **cup peanut butter**
- 2 **Tbsp. sugar**

EQUIPMENT

- **Blender**
- **Measuring cups & spoon**
- **Spatula**

Peanut Butter Milkshakes

You've got milk, peanut butter and probably vanilla ice cream too. Using just a few ingredients, you can whip up this peanut butter milkshake recipe in seconds.
—Joyce Turley, Slaughters, KY

TAKES: 5 min. • **MAKES:** 3 servings

In a blender, combine all the ingredients; cover and process for 30 seconds or until smooth. Stir if necessary. Pour into glasses; serve immediately.

1 CUP 519 cal., 34g fat (12g sat. fat), 47mg chol., 287mg sod., 43g carb. (35g sugars, 3g fiber), 15g pro.

Looking Good.

To get the peanutty rims shown on our glasses, place about ⅓ cup peanut butter in a small bowl (that your serving glasses will still fit into). Microwave the peanut butter to melt, then dip the glasses into peanut butter. If you want, garnish the rims with peanut butter chips, chocolate chips or chopped peanuts while the peanut butter is still warm and soft!

Waffle Fry Nachos

My husband and two grown sons really enjoy these appetizers when we're camping. They can devour a platter of them in no time. The snack is also fun to make when friends come over.
—**Debra Morgan, Idaho Falls, ID**

TAKES: 25 min. • **MAKES:** 8 servings

INGREDIENTS

- 1 pkg. (22 oz.) frozen waffle fries
- 10 bacon strips, cooked and crumbled
- 3 green onions, sliced
- 1 can (6 oz.) sliced ripe olives, drained
- 2 medium tomatoes, seeded and chopped
- ⅔ cup salsa
- 1½ cups shredded cheddar cheese
- 1½ cups shredded Monterey Jack cheese
-    Sour cream

Bake fries according to package directions. Transfer to a 10-in. ovenproof skillet. Top with bacon, onions, olives, tomatoes, salsa and cheeses. Return to oven and bake until cheese is melted, about 5 minutes. Serve with sour cream.

1 CUP 370 cal., 23g fat (12g sat. fat), 48mg chol., 683mg sod., 25g carb. (3g sugars, 4g fiber), 15g pro.

EQUIPMENT

- Baking pans
- 10-in. ovenproof skillet
- Pan & tongs for cooking bacon
- Knife & cutting board
- Measuring cups

How to Quickly Seed a Tomato

Cut tomato in half or into wedges. Use a teaspoon or your fingertip to remove the gel pocket and seeds. Then chop the tomato as desired.

"Dip, dip."
—SOPHIA P., AGE 1

Marshmallow Fruit Dip

You can whip up this sweet and creamy dip in just 10 minutes. I like to serve it in a bowl surrounded by fresh-picked strawberries at spring brunches or luncheons.

—Cindy Steffen, Cedarburg, WI

INGREDIENTS

- 1 pkg. (8 oz.) cream cheese, softened
- ¾ cup cherry yogurt
- 1 carton (8 oz.) frozen whipped topping, thawed
- 1 jar (7 oz.) marshmallow creme
- Assorted fresh fruit

EQUIPMENT

- Large bowl
- Measuring cup
- Mixer or kitchen spoon
- Spatula

TAKES: 10 min. • **MAKES:** 5 cups (40 servings)

In a large bowl, beat cream cheese and yogurt until blended. Using a spatula, fold in whipped topping and marshmallow creme. Serve with fruit.

2 TBSP. 56 cal., 3g fat (2g sat. fat), 7mg chol., 24mg sod., 6g carb. (5g sugars, 0 fiber), 1g pro.

How to Cut Heart-Shaped Berries

Cut a strawberry in half from tip to crown. Then place the half cut side down and cut off the crown with a V-shaped cut. Slice it up and you'll have happy hearts!

SKILL LEVEL 2

Homemade Granola Bars

My husband and I enjoy these bars every day. It's a basic recipe to which you can add any of your favorite flavors. Try them with coconut or different kinds of chips, nuts and dried fruits.

—Jean Boyce, New Ulm, MN

PREP: 15 min. • **BAKE:** 15 min. + cooling • **MAKES:** 3 dozen

INGREDIENTS

- 4 **cups quick-cooking oats**
- 1 **cup packed brown sugar**
- 1 **cup chopped salted peanuts**
- 1 **cup semisweet chocolate chips**
- ½ **cup sunflower kernels**
- ¾ **cup butter, melted**
- ⅔ **cup honey**
- 1 **tsp. vanilla extract**

EQUIPMENT

- **Large bowl**
- **Measuring cups & spoon**
- **Kitchen spoon**
- **15x10x1-in. baking pan**
- **Wire rack**

1. Preheat oven to 350°. In a large bowl, combine oats, brown sugar, peanuts, chocolate chips and sunflower kernels. Stir in butter, honey and vanilla until combined (mixture will be crumbly). Press into a greased parchment-lined 15x10x1-in. baking pan.

2. Bake until lightly browned, 15-20 minutes. Cool 15 minutes in pan on a wire rack; cut into bars. Cool completely before removing from pan.

FREEZE OPTION Transfer cooled bars to an airtight container. Cover and freeze for up to 2 months. To use, thaw bars at room temperature.

1 BAR 167 cal., 9g fat (4g sat. fat), 10mg chol., 54mg sod., 21g carb. (14g sugars, 2g fiber), 3g pro. **DIABETIC EXCHANGES** 1½ starch, 1½ fat.

Everly C. loves getting creative with chocolate.

Create Your Own Flavors

Add your favorite ingredients to create a signature granola bar flavor. Consider raisins, chopped walnuts and cinnamon for an oatmeal cookie-flavored bar. Use chopped dried apricots, pistachios and a little orange zest for a Greek version. Or go nuts with chopped peanuts, peanut butter chips and peanut butter.

"Use chocolate chunks instead of chocolate chips. That way, you get more chocolate in every bite."

–EVERLY C., AGE 7

SKILL LEVEL 1

INGREDIENTS

- 1 cup plain or frosted animal crackers
- 1 cup bear-shaped crackers
- 1 cup miniature pretzels
- 1 cup salted peanuts
- 1 cup M&M's
- 1 cup yogurt- or chocolate-covered raisins

EQUIPMENT

- Bowl
- Measuring cup
- Kitchen spoon

Kiddie Crunch Mix

This no-bake snack mix is a real treat for kids, and you can easily increase the amount to fit your needs. Place in individual plastic bags or pour some into colored ice cream cones and cover with plastic wrap for a fun presentation.

—Kara de la Vega, Santa Rosa, CA

TAKES: 10 min. • **MAKES:** 6 cups

In a bowl, combine all ingredients. Store in an airtight container.

½ CUP 266 cal., 14g fat (5g sat. fat), 4mg chol., 159mg sod., 33g carb. (23g sugars, 3g fiber), 6g pro.

"I made this with my kindergarten class. They loved it! Fun and delicious!"

—CYNANDTOM, TASTEOFHOME.COM

SKILL LEVEL 1

Caramel Apple Float

Who doesn't love the flavors of caramel, apples and vanilla ice cream together? If I'm feeling fancy, I drizzle caramel syrup around the inside of my glass before adding the apple cider and ginger ale.

—Cindy Reams, Philipsburg, PA

INGREDIENTS

1 cup chilled apple cider or unsweetened apple juice

1 cup chilled ginger ale or lemon-lime soda

1 cup vanilla ice cream

2 Tbsp. caramel sundae syrup

Finely chopped peeled apple, optional

EQUIPMENT

- Measuring cup & spoon
- Ice cream scoop

TAKES: 10 min. • **MAKES:** 2 servings

Divide cider and ginger ale between 2 glasses. Top each with ice cream; drizzle with caramel syrup. Add chopped apples if desired.

1 SERVING 220 cal., 4g fat (2g sat. fat), 15mg chol., 102mg sod., 46g carb. (41g sugars, 0 fiber), 2g pro.

Caramel Cuties

Wash and dry **seedless green or red grapes**; add a toothpick to each. Dip each grape in **caramel syrup**, then roll in **nuts or sprinkles**. Chill caramel "apples" to help them set up faster.

SKILL LEVEL 3

Mini Mac & Cheese Bites

Young relatives were coming for a Christmas party, so I wanted something fun for them to eat. Turns out, the adults devoured these tasty bites.

—Kate Mainiero, Elizaville, NY

PREP: 35 min. • **BAKE:** 10 min. • **MAKES:** 3 dozen

INGREDIENTS

- 2 cups uncooked elbow macaroni
- 1 cup seasoned bread crumbs, divided
- 2 Tbsp. butter
- 2 Tbsp. all-purpose flour
- ½ tsp. onion powder
- ½ tsp. garlic powder
- ½ tsp. seasoned salt
- 1¾ cups 2% milk
- 2 cups shredded sharp cheddar cheese, divided
- 1 cup shredded Swiss cheese
- ¾ cup biscuit/baking mix
- 2 large eggs, room temperature, lightly beaten

EQUIPMENT

- Saucepan, kitchen spoon and strainer for cooking macaroni
- Measuring cups & spoons
- Miniature muffin tins
- Large saucepan
- Whisk

1. Preheat oven to 425°. Cook macaroni according to package directions; drain.

2. Meanwhile, sprinkle ¼ cup bread crumbs into 36 greased mini-muffin cups. In a large saucepan, melt butter over medium heat. Stir in flour and seasonings until smooth; gradually whisk in milk. Bring to a boil, stirring constantly; cook and stir until thickened, 1-2 minutes. Stir in 1 cup cheddar cheese and Swiss cheese until melted.

3. Remove from heat; stir in biscuit mix, eggs and ½ cup bread crumbs. Add macaroni; toss to coat. Spoon about 2 Tbsp. macaroni mixture into each prepared mini-muffin cups; sprinkle with remaining cheddar cheese and seasoned bread crumbs.

4. Bake until golden brown, 8-10 minutes. Cool in pans 5 minutes before serving.

1 APPETIZER 91 cal., 5g fat (3g sat. fat), 22mg chol., 162mg sod., 8g carb. (1g sugars, 0 fiber), 4g pro.

It's Science!

Sharp cheddar cheese is like a superhero of flavors. It's aged longer than regular cheddar, which makes it taste stronger! This means you get more cheesy flavor out of each cup of sharp cheddar cheese in your recipe. It's also great for cooking lighter meals because you need less cheese to get the same rich, amazing flavor.

INGREDIENTS

- 4 cups nonfat dry milk powder
- 2 cups white baking chips
- 2 cups baking cocoa
- 1½ cups confectioners' sugar
- ½ tsp. salt

EACH SERVING

- 1 cup hot 2% milk

EQUIPMENT

- Food processor
- Measuring cups & spoon

Double Chocolate Hot Cocoa Mix

I gave this hot cocoa mix away at our neighborhood Christmas party in cute gift bags and was thrilled that I was able to give something to everyone. The next week I started getting calls from the neighbors who'd made it. I was blown by the response! Everyone loves this. The white chocolate is what makes it extra creamy and chocolaty!

—Mandy Rivers, Lexington, SC

TAKES: 10 min. • **MAKES:** 20 servings (6⅔ cups hot cocoa mix)

Pulse the first 5 ingredients in a food processor until baking chips are finely ground. Transfer to a large airtight container. Store in a cool, dry place up to 6 months.

TO PREPARE HOT COCOA Place ⅓ cup hot cocoa mix in a mug. Stir in 1 cup hot milk until blended.

1 CUP PREPARED HOT COCOA 321 cal., 11g fat (6g sat. fat), 25mg chol., 264mg sod., 43g carb. (38g sugars, 2g fiber), 15g pro.

Make It Your Own!

Treat your friends to a DIY hot cocoa bar. They'll love getting creative with these stir-ins and toppings.

- Mini marshmallows
- Ground cinnamon
- Whipped cream
- Caramel sauce
- Chocolate chips

- Sprinkles
- Colored sugars
- Crushed candy canes
- Candy cane or cinnamon stick stirrers

"Chocolate! And milk, please. I like milk."

–EMILY P., AGE 4

PAGE
198

SWEETS & BAKING

SKILL LEVEL 2

INGREDIENTS

- 4 oz. cream cheese, softened
- 4 oz. frozen whipped topping, thawed
- ½ tsp. vanilla extract
- 3 Tbsp. confectioners' sugar
- 1 round slice of whole seedless watermelon, about 1 in. thick

  Assorted fresh fruit

  Fresh mint leaves, optional

EQUIPMENT

- **Small bowl**
- **Mixer or kitchen spoon**
- **Spatula**
- **Measuring spoons**
- **Knife & cutting board**
- **Offset spatula**

Watermelon Fruit Pizza

Fruit pizza is an easy and refreshing way to end a summer meal. Top it with any fruit you may have on hand, and add other toppings like fresh mint, toasted shredded coconut or chopped nuts.
—*Taste of Home* Test Kitchen

TAKES: 10 min. • **MAKES:** 8 servings

1. In a small bowl, beat cream cheese until smooth. Gently fold in whipped topping, then vanilla and confectioners' sugar until combined.

2. To serve, spread watermelon slice with cream cheese mixture. Cut into 8 wedges and top with your fruit of choice. If desired, garnish pizza with fresh mint.

1 PIECE 140 cal., 7g fat (5g sat. fat), 14mg chol., 45mg sod., 17g carb. (16g sugars, 0 fiber), 1g pro. **DIABETIC EXCHANGES** 1½ fat, 1 fruit.

Looking Good.

Unlike ordinary pizza, this one is "sauced," then cut, before adding the toppings. Cutting the pizza first means each slice is pretty and you won't have to cut through a berry or otherwise disturb the fruity toppings.

"Baking chocolate chip cookies is a special experience for my daughters and me. We use the same Kitchen-Aid mixer my grandmother and I used when I was a little girl."
—SAMANTHA H., MOM

Annie H., age 8, and her mom, Samantha, make their cookies with the best chocolate chips Samantha can find.

SKILL LEVEL 1

Big & Buttery Chocolate Chip Cookies

Our version of the classic cookie is based on a recipe from a California bakery called Hungry Bear. The cookie is big, thick and chewy—perfect for dunking.

—Irene Yeh, Mequon, WI

PREP: 35 min. + chilling • **BAKE:** 10 min./batch • **MAKES:** about 2 dozen

INGREDIENTS

- 1 cup butter, softened
- 1 cup packed brown sugar
- ¾ cup sugar
- 2 large eggs, room temperature
- 1½ tsp. vanilla extract
- 2⅔ cups all-purpose flour
- 1¼ tsp. baking soda
- 1 tsp. salt
- 1 pkg. (12 oz.) semisweet chocolate chips
- 2 cups coarsely chopped walnuts, toasted

EQUIPMENT

- Bowls
- Measuring cups & spoons
- Mixer or kitchen spoon
- Airtight container
- Baking sheets
- Wire racks

1. In a large bowl, beat butter and sugars until blended. Beat in eggs and vanilla. In a small bowl, combine flour, baking soda and salt; gradually beat into butter mixture. Stir in chocolate chips and walnuts.

2. Shape ¼ cupfuls of dough into balls. Flatten each to ¾-in. thickness (2½ in. diameter), smoothing edge as necessary. Place in an airtight container, separating layers with waxed paper or parchment; refrigerate, covered, overnight.

3. To bake, place dough portions 2 in. apart on parchment-lined baking sheets; let stand at room temperature 30 minutes before baking. Preheat oven to 400°.

4. Bake 10-12 minutes or until edges are golden brown (centers will be light). Cool on pans 2 minutes. Remove cookies to wire racks to cool.

NOTE To toast nuts, bake in a shallow pan in a 350°; oven for 5-10 minutes or cook in a skillet over low heat until lightly browned, stirring occasionally.

1 COOKIE 311 cal., 19g fat (8g sat. fat), 38mg chol., 229mg sod., 35g carb. (23g sugars, 2g fiber), 4g pro.

How to Keep Cookies Soft

Add a slice of white bread to the container to preserve the moisture of your stored cookies.

SKILL LEVEL 3

Angel Food Cake Roll

There's always room for dessert—especially when it's this eye-catching frozen fare. We like strawberry yogurt in the filling, but other flavors work well too.

—Joan Colbert, Sigourney, IA

PREP: 30 min. + freezing • **BAKE:** 15 min. + cooling • **MAKES:** 12 servings

INGREDIENTS

- 1 **pkg. (16 oz.) angel food cake mix**
- **Confectioners' sugar**
- 1 **cup strawberry yogurt**
- 1 **pkg. (3.4 oz.) instant vanilla pudding mix**
- 3 **drops red food coloring, optional**
- 2 **cups whipped topping**

EQUIPMENT

- **15x10x1-in. baking pan**
- **Bowls**
- **Measuring cups**
- **Mixer or kitchen spoon**
- **Clean tea towel**
- **Wire rack**
- **Whisk**
- **Offset spatula**

1. Preheat oven to 350°. Line an ungreased 15x10x1-in. baking pan with parchment.

2. Prepare cake batter according to package directions. Transfer to prepared pan. Bake until top springs back when lightly touched, 15-20 minutes. Cool 5 minutes. Invert onto a tea towel dusted with confectioners' sugar. Gently peel off paper. Roll up cake in the towel, jelly-roll style, starting with a short side. Cool completely on a wire rack.

3. Whisk together yogurt, pudding mix and, if desired, food coloring. Fold in whipped topping.

4. Unroll cake. Using an offset spatula, spread yogurt mixture over cake to within ½ in. of edges. Roll up again, without towel. Cover tightly and freeze. Remove from freezer 30 minutes before slicing.

1 PIECE 243 cal., 3g fat (3g sat. fat), 1mg chol., 427mg sod., 50g carb. (37g sugars, 0 fiber), 4g pro.

How to Make a Cake Roll

Place clean towel on a wire rack. Use a shaker or strainer to dust the towel well with confectioners' sugar. (This prevents sticking.) Then gently roll it up and let cool. Be careful not to overbake your cake, or it may crack. If the cake does crack or break up when you roll it, you can disguise the mistake with frosting or whipped cream.

SKILL LEVEL
2

INGREDIENTS

- 3 Tbsp. chocolate hard-shell ice cream topping
- 1 graham cracker crust (9 in.)
- 2 medium bananas, sliced
- ½ tsp. lemon juice
- ½ cup pineapple ice cream topping
- 1 qt. strawberry ice cream, softened
- 2 cups whipped topping
- ½ cup chopped walnuts, toasted
   Chocolate syrup
- 8 maraschino cherries with stems

EQUIPMENT

- Measuring cups & spoons
- Knife & cutting board
- Small bowl
- Kitchen spoon

Frozen Banana Split Pie

This dessert is special enough to make hamburgers and fries a meal to remember! It's so tall and pretty, and it is just like eating a frozen banana split. Make it ahead to save time.

—Joy Collins, Birmingham, AL

PREP: 25 min. + freezing • **MAKES:** 8 servings

1. Pour topping into crust; freeze 5 minutes or until firm.

2. Meanwhile, place bananas in a small bowl; toss with lemon juice. Arrange bananas over hardened topping. Layer with pineapple topping, ice cream, whipped topping and walnuts.

3. Cover and freeze until firm. Remove from the freezer 15 minutes before cutting. Garnish with chocolate syrup and cherries.

1 PIECE 459 cal., 22g fat (9g sat. fat), 19mg chol., 174mg sod., 64g carb. (26g sugars, 2g fiber), 5g pro.

Make It Your Own!

SWAP ICE CREAM FLAVORS. Instead of strawberry, try vanilla ice cream, butter pecan or raspberry ripple. Avoid supersweet flavors, or the pie might taste too sugary.

LAYER THE FLAVORS. You can add a thin layer of chocolate, strawberry and vanilla ice creams to make a striking layered pie. Freeze each layer for an hour before adding the next.

CHANGE THE TOPPINGS. Consider caramel topping, chopped pecans or your favorite candies to finish off this masterpiece.

SKILL LEVEL 3

INGREDIENTS

1 cup whole wheat flour

¾ cup all-purpose flour

½ cup toasted wheat germ

2 Tbsp. dark brown sugar

1 tsp. baking powder

1 tsp. ground cinnamon

½ tsp. salt

½ tsp. baking soda

6 Tbsp. cold butter, cubed

¼ cup honey

4 Tbsp. ice water

EQUIPMENT

• Bowls

• Measuring cups & spoons

• Whisk

• Pastry blender or 2 forks

• Fork

• Rolling pin

• Ruler

• Knife, fluted pastry wheel or pizza cutter

• Baking sheets

• Wire racks

Homemade Honey Grahams

The way my boys eat them, I would spend a fortune on honey graham crackers at the grocery store. My homemade version is less expensive—and less processed. These are wonderful, although they still don't last long.
—Crystal Jo Bruns, Iliff, CO

PREP: 15 min. + chilling • **BAKE:** 10 min./batch • **MAKES:** 32 crackers

1. In a bowl, whisk first 8 ingredients. Using a pastry blender or 2 forks, cut in butter until crumbly. In another bowl, whisk honey and water; gradually add to dry ingredients, tossing with a fork until dough holds together when pressed. Shape dough into 2 flattened portions; cover and refrigerate until firm enough to roll, about 30 minutes.

2. Preheat oven to 350°. On a lightly floured surface, roll each portion of dough to an 8-in. square. Using a knife or fluted pastry wheel, cut each portion into sixteen 2-in. squares. If desired, prick holes with a fork. Place 1 in. apart on parchment-lined baking sheets.

3. Bake until edges are light brown, 10-12 minutes. Remove from pans to wire racks to cool. Store in an airtight container.

1 CRACKER 60 cal., 2g fat (1g sat. fat), 6mg chol., 89mg sod., 9g carb. (3g sugars, 1g fiber), 1g pro. **DIABETIC EXCHANGES** ½ starch, ½ fat.

> **"The first rule of mixing: Don't fling! You have to stir carefully so the dry ingredients don't fly out of the bowl."**
> —AIDEN S., AGE 14

SKILL LEVEL 3

Cream-Filled Cupcakes

These chocolate cupcakes have a fun filling and shiny frosting that make them super special. They're always gone in no time!
—Kathy Kittell, Lenexa, KS

INGREDIENTS

- 1 pkg. devil's food cake mix (regular size)
- 2 tsp. hot water
- ¼ tsp. salt
- 1 jar (7 oz.) marshmallow creme
- ½ cup shortening
- ⅓ cup confectioners' sugar
- ½ tsp. vanilla extract

GANACHE FROSTING

- 1 cup semisweet chocolate chips
- ¾ cup heavy whipping cream

PREP: 30 min. • **BAKE:** 15 min. + cooling • **MAKES:** 2 dozen

1. Prepare and bake cake batter according to package directions, using 24 paper-lined muffin cups. Cool for 5 minutes before removing from pans to wire racks to cool completely.

2. For filling, in a small bowl, combine water and salt until salt is dissolved. Cool. In a small bowl, beat the marshmallow creme, shortening, confectioners' sugar and vanilla until light and fluffy; beat in the salt mixture.

3. Transfer cream filling to a pastry bag fitted with a round pastry tip. Push tip through the top of each cupcake to fill center.

4. Place chocolate chips in a small bowl. In a small saucepan, bring cream just to a boil. Pour over chocolate; whisk until smooth. Cool, stirring occasionally, to room temperature or until ganache reaches a dipping consistency.

5. Dip cupcake tops in ganache; refrigerate for 20 minutes or until set. Decorate with Vanilla Icing (recipe below) if desired. Store in the refrigerator.

1 CUPCAKE 262 cal., 15g fat (5g sat. fat), 32mg chol., 223mg sod., 29g carb. (20g sugars, 1g fiber), 2g pro.

Vanilla Icing

Mix together ½ cup **confectioners' sugar**, 2 Tbsp. softened **butter**, 1½ tsp. **milk** and ¼ tsp. **vanilla extract**. Place in a small piping bag with round tip and decorate cupcakes. You can make shapes, faces or letters to spell a friend's name.

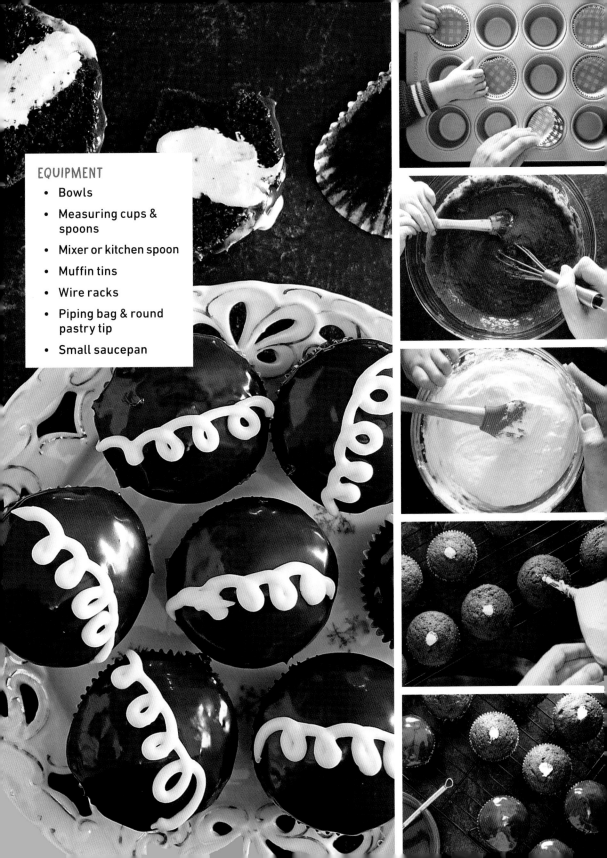

EQUIPMENT

- Bowls
- Measuring cups & spoons
- Mixer or kitchen spoon
- Muffin tins
- Wire racks
- Piping bag & round pastry tip
- Small saucepan

"My kids first started helping me bake by measuring the dry ingredients. Still, when we bake together, we split up the work by who will measure the wet and who will measure the dry ingredients. Mom usually does the dishes, unfortunately."

—PEGGY W., MOM

SKILL LEVEL **1**

Blueberry Bread

This is a simple quick bread recipe that I look forward to making when fresh blueberries are in season. It's so good, though, that I end up making it year-round.

—Karen Scales, Waukesha, WI

INGREDIENTS

- 2 cups plus 2 Tbsp. all-purpose flour, divided
- ¾ cup sugar
- 1 tsp. baking powder
- ½ tsp. salt
- ¼ tsp. baking soda
- 1 large egg, room temperature
- ⅔ cup orange juice
- 2 Tbsp. butter, melted
- 1 cup fresh or frozen blueberries

EQUIPMENT

- Bowls
- Measuring cups & spoons
- Whisk
- Kitchen spoon
- 8x4-in. loaf pan
- Wire rack

PREP: 10 min. • **BAKE:** 1 hour + cooling • **MAKES:** 1 loaf (12 pieces)

1. Preheat oven to 325°. In a large bowl, whisk 2 cups flour, sugar, baking powder, salt and baking soda. Whisk the egg, orange juice and butter. Stir into dry ingredients just until moistened. Toss blueberries with remaining flour; fold into batter.

2. Pour into a greased 8x4-in. loaf pan. Bake until a toothpick inserted in the center comes out clean, 60-65 minutes. Cool in pan for 10 minutes before removing to a wire rack to cool completely.

NOTE If using frozen blueberries, use without thawing to avoid discoloring the batter.

1 PIECE 165 cal., 3g fat (1g sat. fat), 21mg chol., 186mg sod., 33g carb. (15g sugars, 1g fiber), 3g pro. **DIABETIC EXCHANGES** 2 starch, ½ fat.

Berry Snack Parfaits

Beat 4 oz. softened **cream cheese** with 3 Tbsp. **sugar**. Fold in 1⅓ cups **sweetened whipped cream or whipped topping**. Layer with **fresh berries** in 4 dessert dishes.

INGREDIENTS

- 1 **yellow cake mix (regular size)**
- 1 **large egg, room temperature**
- ½ **cup 2% milk**
- ⅓ **cup canola oil**
- 1 **cup white baking chips**
- ⅓ **cup jimmies**

EQUIPMENT

- **Large bowl**
- **Measuring cups**
- **Kitchen spoon**
- **15x10x1-in. baking pan**
- **Wire rack**

Easy Cake Mix Bars

I take these bars to work for Friday pick-me-ups. I love to share them because they're so easy to eat, easy to make and easy on the wallet.

—Amy Rose, Ballwin, MO

PREP: 5 min. • **BAKE:** 20 min. + cooling • **MAKES:** 3 dozen

1. Preheat oven to 350°. In a large bowl, combine cake mix, egg, milk and oil (mixture will be thick). Stir in baking chips and jimmies. Spread into a greased 15x10x1-in. baking pan.

2. Bake 18-20 minutes or until a toothpick inserted in center comes out clean. Cool completely in pan on a wire rack. Cut into bars.

FREEZE OPTION Freeze bars in freezer containers. To use, thaw in covered containers before serving.

1 BAR 113 cal., 5g fat (2g sat. fat), 7mg chol., 102mg sod., 16g carb. (11g sugars, 0 fiber), 1g pro.

"Quick and easy. This is a good recipe for little kids. My 3-year-old added the ingredients and helped with the mixing."

—CHRIS_GILES18, TASTEOFHOME.COM

SKILL LEVEL 2

No-Bake Cookies

INGREDIENTS

- 2 cups sugar
- ½ cup fat-free milk
- ½ cup butter, cubed
- 3 cups quick-cooking oats
- 1 cup sweetened shredded coconut
- 6 Tbsp. baking cocoa
- ½ tsp. vanilla extract

EQUIPMENT

- **Large saucepan**
- **Measuring cups & spoons**
- **Kitchen spoon**

This is my son's all-time favorite cookie. He will share just about anything, but these are an exception ... he gobbles them up! They travel well in a lunchbox too.
—**Carol Brandon, Uxbridge, ON**

PREP: 10 min. + standing • **MAKES:** 3 dozen

1. In a large saucepan, combine the sugar, milk and butter; bring to a boil, stirring constantly. Boil for 2 minutes.

2. Remove from heat. Stir in the oats, coconut, cocoa and vanilla.

3. Working quickly, drop by rounded tablespoonfuls onto waxed paper. Let stand until set, about 1 hour.

1 COOKIE 107 cal., 4g fat (3g sat. fat), 7mg chol., 29mg sod., 18g carb. (13g sugars, 1g fiber), 1g pro.

Chocolate & Peanut Butter No-Bake Cookies After Step 1, stir ½ cup peanut butter into the mixture until blended. Proceed as directed.

It's Science!

If you ever have a batch of these turn out hard, it's because you cooked the sugar mixture too long. Sugar boils at a high temperature, and the hotter it gets, the harder it becomes when cool. Think about soft, chewy taffy vs. hard candy canes: The candy canes were cooked to a higher temperature. As soon as your sugar mixture comes to a boil, start a timer for 2 minutes.

Grainy cookies are another problem. To avoid those, stir constantly until the mixture comes to a boil.

How to Give 'Em a Kiss

Just before baking, gently push the point of an unwrapped kiss into each muffin cup. Get creative with other flavors of kisses, such as birthday cake or cookies 'n' creme.

SKILL LEVEL
1

Brownie Kiss Cupcakes

It's fun to make these individual brownie cupcakes with a chocolaty surprise inside. My goddaughter asked me to make them for her birthday to share with classmates at school. She requested 32 treats. I later found out she needed only 27. I wonder where the other five went!

—Pamela Lute, Mercersburg, PA

TAKES: 30 min. • **MAKES:** 9 cupcakes

INGREDIENTS

⅓ **cup butter, softened**

1 **cup sugar**

2 **large eggs, room temperature**

1 **tsp. vanilla extract**

¾ **cup all-purpose flour**

½ **cup baking cocoa**

¼ **tsp. baking powder**

¼ **tsp. salt**

9 **milk chocolate kisses**

EQUIPMENT

- **Bowls**
- **Measuring cups & spoons**
- **Mixer or kitchen spoon**
- **Muffin tin**

1. Preheat oven to 350°. In a large bowl, cream butter and sugar until light and fluffy, 5-7 minutes. Beat in the eggs and vanilla. Combine the flour, cocoa, baking powder and salt; gradually add to the creamed mixture and mix well.

2. Fill 9 paper- or foil-lined muffin cups two-thirds full. Place 1 chocolate kiss tip end down in the center of each.

3. Bake until top of brownie springs back when lightly touched, 20-25 minutes.

1 CUPCAKE 239 cal., 10g fat (5g sat. fat), 66mg chol., 163mg sod., 36g carb. (24g sugars, 1g fiber), 4g pro.

A Regular Favorite

"This recipe is a favorite of our almost-10-year-old grandson, Karsten. We started making them when he was about 5, and he still asks Grams if we can make his favorite 'brown cupcakes.'"
—Sue G., grandma

Karsten K., age 4 here, has made these small-batch cupcakes for years with his grandma.

Bake-Sale Lemon Bars

The recipe for these tangy lemon bars comes from my cousin, who is famous for cooking up farm feasts.

—Mildred Keller, Rockford, IL

INGREDIENTS

- ¾ cup butter, softened
- ⅔ cup confectioners' sugar
- 1½ cups plus 3 Tbsp. all-purpose flour, divided
- 3 large eggs
- 1½ cups sugar
- ¼ cup lemon juice
- Additional confectioners' sugar

PREP: 25 min. • **BAKE:** 20 min. + cooling • **MAKES:** 15 bars

1. Preheat oven to 350°. In a large bowl, beat butter and confectioners' sugar until blended. Gradually beat in 1½ cups flour. Press onto bottom of a greased 13x9-in. baking pan. Bake 18-20 minutes or until golden brown.

2. Meanwhile, in a small bowl, whisk eggs, sugar, lemon juice and remaining flour until frothy; carefully pour over hot crust.

3. Bake for 20-25 minutes or until lemon mixture is set and lightly browned. Cool completely on a wire rack. Dust with additional confectioners' sugar. Cut into bars. Refrigerate leftovers.

1 BAR 247 cal., 10g fat (6g sat. fat), 62mg chol., 88mg sod., 37g carb. (26g sugars, 0 fiber), 3g pro.

How to Juice a Lemon Without a Juicer

STEP 1: Roll a lemon on the counter 20 seconds, using a good amount of force. This helps release the juices.

STEP 2: Using a skewer, poke the non-stem end of the lemon—the end that's a little pointed. Push the skewer in at least 1 in., being careful not to poke it all the way through.

STEP 3: Turn the poked end over a bowl and squeeze. A medium lemon will yield 2 to 3 Tbsp. of juice.

NOTE: You can use bottled juice in this recipe, but fresh tastes better. For more lemony flavor, zest the lemons with a rasp or the fine side of a box grater before juicing. Add zest to the egg mixture.

EQUIPMENT

- Bowls
- Measuring cups & spoon
- Mixer or kitchen spoon
- 13x9-in. baking pan
- Whisk
- Wire rack

"My favorite part of cooking is having fun and tasting the masterpiece I made after I'm finished."
—MADELEINE B., AGE 10

SKILL LEVEL 1

Chunky Banana Cream Freeze

Everyone loves ice cream, but we all know it doesn't make a great after-school snack. Until this! With its sweet banana-almond flavor and chunky texture, this appealing frozen dessert is a crowd-pleaser. People who ask me for the recipe can't believe how easy it is to make.

—Kristen Bloom, Okinawa, Japan

PREP: 15 min. + freezing • **MAKES:** 6 servings (3 cups)

INGREDIENTS

5 **medium bananas, peeled and frozen**

⅓ **cup almond milk**

2 **Tbsp. unsweetened finely shredded coconut**

2 **Tbsp. creamy peanut butter**

1 **tsp. vanilla extract**

¼ **cup chopped walnuts**

3 **Tbsp. raisins**

EQUIPMENT

• **Food processor**

• **Measuring cups & spoons**

• **Spatula**

• **Kitchen spoon**

1. Place the bananas, milk, coconut, peanut butter and vanilla in a food processor; cover and process until blended.

2. Transfer to a freezer container; stir in walnuts and raisins. Freeze for 2-4 hours before serving.

NOTE Look for unsweetened coconut in the baking or health food section. Regular sweetened coconut will work fine too.

½ CUP 181 cal., 7g fat (2g sat. fat), 0 chol., 35mg sod., 29g carb. (16g sugars, 4g fiber), 3g pro. **DIABETIC EXCHANGES** 1 fruit, 1 fat, ½ starch.

How to Keep Bananas Fresh

To slow ripening, you can wrap plastic or tape around the banana stems. If you can't use them all in time, you can freeze bananas for smoothies, ice cream and other recipes. Peel them, place in a freezer-safe container, and label with the date. Some people freeze bananas with the peel on, but it can be messier and harder to remove the peel later.

SKILL LEVEL 1

INGREDIENTS

- 2 cups sugar
- 1¾ cups all-purpose flour
- ½ cup baking cocoa
- 1 tsp. salt
- 5 large eggs, room temperature
- 1 cup canola oil
- 1 tsp. vanilla extract
- 1 cup semisweet chocolate chips

EQUIPMENT

- Large bowl
- Measuring cups & spoon
- Mixer or kitchen spoon
- 13x9-in. baking pan
- Wire rack

Speedy Brownies

Since you dump all the ingredients together for these brownies, they take very little time to prepare. There's no mistaking the homemade goodness of a freshly baked batch—they are rich and fudgy!
—**Diane Heier, Harwood, ND**

PREP: 15 min. • **BAKE:** 30 min. • **MAKES:** about 3 dozen

1. In a large bowl, beat the first 7 ingredients. Pour into a greased 13x9-in. baking pan. Sprinkle with chocolate chips.

2. Bake at 350° for 30 minutes or until a toothpick inserted in the center comes out clean. Cool in pan on a wire rack.

1 BROWNIE 155 cal., 8g fat (2g sat. fat), 30mg chol., 75mg sod., 19g carb. (14g sugars, 1g fiber), 2g pro.

> **"This was one of the first recipes my sister and I started making by ourselves."**
> **–JACK W., AGE 13**

SKILL LEVEL 2

INGREDIENTS

- 1 pkg. (3 oz.) orange gelatin
- 1 cup boiling water
- 1 cup vanilla yogurt
- ½ cup 2% milk
- ½ tsp. vanilla extract

EQUIPMENT

- • Large bowl
- • Measuring cups & spoon
- • Kitchen spoon
- • Pop molds & sticks

Orange Cream Pops

For a lighter alternative to ice cream pops, try this citrus novelty. The tangy orange flavor will make your taste buds tingle, while the silky smooth texture offers cool comfort.
—*Taste of Home* **Test Kitchen**

PREP: 10 min. + freezing • **MAKES:** 10 pops

In a large bowl, dissolve gelatin in boiling water. Cool to room temperature. Stir in yogurt, milk and vanilla. Pour ¼ cup mixture into each pop mold. Place pop sticks. Freeze until firm.

1 POP 58 cal., 1g fat (0 sat. fat), 2mg chol., 41mg sod., 11g carb. (11g sugars, 0 fiber), 2g pro. **DIABETIC EXCHANGES** 1 starch.

How to Unmold Pops

Run the outside of the pop molds under cold water to help loosen the pops. Jiggle the sticks to work the pops free. Instead of using running water, you can dip the mold into a bowl or glass of water.

"The most important ingredient is love."
—AIDEN S., AGE 14

EQUIPMENT

- Bowls
- Measuring cups & spoons
- Mixer or kitchen spoons
- Zesting tool
- Spatula
- Muffin tins
- Wire racks
- Offset spatula or butter knife

SKILL LEVEL 3

Lemon Coconut Cupcakes

Lemon plus coconut equals big smiles in this cupcake equation.

—**Debra Henderson, Booneville, AR**

INGREDIENTS

- ¾ cup butter, softened
- 1 cup sugar
- 3 large eggs, room temperature
- 3 tsp. grated lemon zest
- ½ tsp. vanilla extract
- 1½ cups all-purpose flour
- ½ tsp. baking powder
- ½ tsp. baking soda
- ¼ tsp. salt
- ½ cup sour cream
- ½ cup sweetened shredded coconut

LEMON COCONUT FROSTING

- 4 oz. cream cheese, softened
- 2 Tbsp. butter, softened
- 1 tsp. grated lemon zest
- ¼ tsp. vanilla extract
- ¼ tsp. lemon juice
- 1¼ cups confectioners' sugar
- ¾ cup sweetened shredded coconut, divided
  Lemon slices, optional

PREP: 20 min. • **BAKE:** 20 min. + cooling • **MAKES:** 15 cupcakes

1. Preheat oven to 350°. In a large bowl, cream butter and sugar until light and fluffy, 5-7 minutes. Add eggs, 1 at a time, beating well after each addition. Beat in lemon zest and vanilla. Combine flour, baking powder, baking soda and salt; add to the creamed mixture alternately with sour cream. Beat just until combined. Fold in coconut.

2. Fill paper-lined muffin cups three-fourths full. Bake until a toothpick comes out clean, 18-22 minutes. Cool for 10 minutes before removing from pans to wire racks to cool completely.

3. In a small bowl, beat the cream cheese, butter, lemon zest, vanilla and lemon juice until fluffy. Gradually beat in confectioners' sugar; stir in ¼ cup coconut. Frost cupcakes; sprinkle with remaining coconut. If desired, garnish with lemon.

1 CUPCAKE 327 cal., 18g fat (12g sat. fat), 85mg chol., 262mg sod., 37g carb. (26g sugars, 1g fiber), 4g pro.

Aiden S. put two people's favorite flavors into one fancy cake for them to share.

A Marriage of Flavors

"Aiden is technically my stepson, but since his dad and I met when he was just 3 years old, I consider him my son. His dad and I got married on April 16, 2020, in the height of the pandemic. We couldn't have the wedding we'd planned, so we got married by the mayor at an outdoor wedding. Aiden was the best man for his dad, the stylist for me, the ring bearer *and* the cake baker! My favorite is coconut and his dad's is lemon, so Aiden made a delicious white cake with lemon zest and coconut on top." —Jody R., mom

Sugared Doughnut Holes

These tasty, tender doughnut bites are easy to make. Tuck them in a pretty box and tie with a bow to give as a party favor.
—Judy Jungwirth, Athol, SD

INGREDIENTS

1½ cups all-purpose flour

⅓ cup sugar

2 tsp. baking powder

½ tsp. salt

½ tsp. ground nutmeg

1 large egg, room temperature

½ cup 2% milk

2 Tbsp. butter, melted

Oil for deep-fat frying

Confectioners' sugar

EQUIPMENT

- Bowls
- Measuring cups & spoons
- Kitchen spoons
- Electric skillet or deep-fat fryer

TAKES: 20 min. • **MAKES:** about 3 dozen

1. In a large bowl, combine flour, sugar, baking powder, salt and nutmeg. In a small bowl, combine egg, milk and butter. Add to dry ingredients and mix well.

2. In an electric skillet or deep-fat fryer, heat oil to 375°. Drop dough by heaping teaspoonfuls, 5 or 6 at a time, into oil. Fry until browned, 1-2 minutes, turning once. Drain on paper towels. Roll warm doughnut holes in confectioners' sugar.

1 DOUGHNUT HOLE 47 cal., 2g fat (1g sat. fat), 7mg chol., 68mg sod., 6g carb. (2g sugars, 0 fiber), 1g pro.

The Game Plan

LITTLE KIDS CAN …
Gather food and equipment, crack the egg and roll warm doughnut holes in confectioners' sugar.

BIG KIDS CAN …
Melt the butter, mix the dough and help the adult cook and turn the doughnut holes.

Cherry Cheesecake

INGREDIENTS

- 11 oz. cream cheese, softened
- 1 cup confectioners' sugar
- 1 carton (8 oz.) frozen whipped topping, thawed
- 1 shortbread or graham cracker crust (9 in.)
- 1 can (21 oz.) cherry pie filling

EQUIPMENT

- Bowl
- Measuring cup
- Mixer or kitchen spoon
- Spatula
- Spoon

When I worked full time and needed a quick dessert to take to a potluck or a friend's home, this pie was always the answer. You can substitute a graham cracker crust or use another type of fruit pie filling for a change of pace. Even the chilling time is flexible if you're in a big hurry.

—Mary Smith, Bradenton, FL

PREP: 15 min. + chilling • **MAKES:** 8 servings

In a bowl, beat the cream cheese and sugar until smooth. With a spatula, fold in whipped topping. Place filling in crust. Top with pie filling. Refrigerate until serving.

1 PIECE 464 cal., 24g fat (14g sat. fat), 43mg chol., 250mg sod., 57g carb. (46g sugars, 1g fiber), 4g pro.

"So easy and so good! I used blueberry pie filling with a graham cracker crust."

—CLASSICROCK, TASTEOFHOME.COM

How to Top the Cheesecake

Gently spoon the pie filling onto your cheesecake, a little at a time. Spread it a bit as you go. This will give you a nice appearance and keep the topping from sinking down into the filling.

SKILL LEVEL 3

Unicorn Mane Cookies

Everyone loves a classic shortbread cookie. Make each cookie magical with a quick dip into melted baking chips and rainbow-colored sprinkles. Your unicorns will love these rainbow bites.

—Angela Lemoine, Howell, NJ

INGREDIENTS

- ½ cup butter, softened
- ¾ cup confectioners' sugar
- 1 large egg, room temperature
- 1½ cups all-purpose flour
- ¼ cup sprinkles
- ½ cup white baking chips, melted
- Additional sprinkles

EQUIPMENT

- Bowls
- Measuring cups
- Mixer or kitchen soon
- Baking sheet
- Rolling pin
- Ruler
- Knife, pastry wheel or pizza cutter
- Wire rack

PREP: 15 min. + chilling • **BAKE:** 10 min. + cooling • **MAKES:** 24 cookies

1. In large bowl, cream butter and confectioners' sugar until light and fluffy, 3-4 minutes. Beat in egg. Gradually add flour until blended. Stir in sprinkles. Form dough into a disk; cover and refrigerate 1 hour.

2. Preheat oven to 375°. Line a baking sheet with parchment. Place dough on parchment and roll into a 12x8-in. rectangle. Score the dough into 24 rectangles. Bake until edges are golden brown, 10-15 minutes. Remove to a wire rack; cool.

3. Break or cut along score marks. Dip 1 edge of each cookie into melted chips, then dip into additional sprinkles; place on waxed paper until set.

1 COOKIE 97 cal., 5g fat (3g sat. fat), 18mg chol., 35mg sod., 12g carb. (6g sugars, 0 fiber), 1g pro.

Make It Your Own!

Mix up the sprinkle colors for different holidays, or decorate the cookies with heart-shaped sprinkles or stars.

Cookies & Cream Bark

This is an easy bark to make that everyone will enjoy. Swap in any of the holiday-flavored cookies you like to create a more festive candy.

—James Schend,
  Pleasant Prairie, WI

INGREDIENTS

- 1 pkg. (10 to 12 oz.) white baking chips
- 15 Oreo cookies, crushed (1½ cups), divided

EQUIPMENT

- **15x10-in. pan**
- **Metal bowl that fits over a pot of hot water or microwave-safe bowl**
- **Kitchen spoon**
- **Measuring cups**

PREP: 20 min. + chilling • **MAKES:** about 1 lb.

1. Line a 15x10x1-in. pan with parchment; set aside.

2. In a metal bowl over hot water, melt the baking chips until two-thirds are melted. Stir until smooth. Stir in ¾ cup crushed cookies. Spread into prepared pan; top with remaining cookies (pan will not be full). Refrigerate until firm, 15-20 minutes. Break or cut into pieces. Store in an airtight container.

1 OZ. 153 cal., 8g fat (4g sat. fat), 4mg chol., 82mg sod., 19g carb. (15g sugars, 1g fiber), 2g pro.

How to Melt Chocolate Chips in a Microwave

Microwave at 70% power for 30 seconds. Remove from microwave and stir. Continue to microwave in 15-second increments, stirring each time, until the chocolate is melted. Be especially careful with white chocolate; it can overcook and become grainy.

"When my dad and I bake bread together, I get to measure and punch down the dough."

—ROWAN C., AGE 9

SKILL LEVEL 3

Buttery Bubble Bread

Homemade bread can be time-consuming, difficult and tricky to make. But this fun-to-eat monkey bread, baked in a Bundt pan, is easy and almost foolproof. If I'm serving it for breakfast, I add some cinnamon and drizzle it with icing.

—Pat Stevens, Granbury, TX

PREP: 25 min. + rising • **BAKE:** 30 min. • **MAKES:** 16 servings

INGREDIENTS

- 1 pkg. (¼ oz.) active dry yeast
- 1 cup warm water (110° to 115°)
- ½ cup sugar
- ½ cup shortening
- 1 large egg, room temperature
- ½ tsp. salt
- 4 to 4½ cups all-purpose flour, divided
- 6 Tbsp. butter, melted

EQUIPMENT

- Large bowls
- Measuring cups & spoon
- Mixer or kitchen spoon
- Small bowl for melted butter
- 9-in. Bundt pan

1. In a large bowl, dissolve yeast in warm water. Add the sugar, shortening, egg, salt and 1 cup of flour. Beat until smooth. Stir in enough remaining flour to form a soft dough.

2. Turn onto a floured surface; knead until smooth and elastic, 6-8 minutes. Place in a greased bowl, turning once to grease top. Cover and let rise in a warm place until doubled, about 1 hour.

3. Punch dough down. Turn onto a lightly floured surface; shape into 1½-in. balls. Dip the balls in butter and arrange evenly in a greased 9-in. Bundt pan. Drizzle with the remaining butter. Cover and let rise in a warm place until doubled, about 45 minutes.

4. Bake at 350° for 30-35 minutes or until golden brown. Cool for 5 minutes before inverting onto a serving platter. Serve warm.

1 SERVING 237 cal., 11g fat (4g sat. fat), 25mg chol., 122mg sod., 30g carb. (7g sugars, 1g fiber), 4g pro.

Punch Time

Punching down dough is satisfying and fun. But how do you know when it's time to punch? Recipe rise times are only a guide. Dough rises more slowly in a cool place or if it's made with older yeast. Judge the dough by its size (if it's doubled or nearly doubled), and if it holds an indentation when gently pressed.

Rowan C.'s dough is at the perfect spot for punching.

INGREDIENTS

- 24 ice cream cake cones (about 3 in. tall)
- 1 pkg. French vanilla or yellow cake mix (regular size)

FROSTING

- 1 cup butter, softened
- ½ cup shortening
- 6 cups confectioners' sugar
- ¼ cup 2% milk
- 2 tsp. vanilla extract

GLAZE

- 4 cups semisweet chocolate chips
- ¼ cup shortening
- Colored sprinkles

EQUIPMENT

- Mini muffin tins
- Bowls
- Measuring cups & spoon
- Mixer or kitchen spoon
- Wire racks
- Small offset spatula
- Metal bowl and pan for melting chocolate

Chocolate-Dipped Ice Cream Cone Cupcakes

I created this recipe based on our family's love of chocolate-dipped ice cream cones. Red heart-shaped sprinkles make them fun for Valentine's Day. Vary the color to match the occasion.
—Jennifer Gilbert, Brighton, MI

PREP: 50 min. • **BAKE:** 15 min. + cooling • **MAKES:** 2 dozen

1. Preheat oven to 350°. Grease 24 mini-muffin cups. Stand ice cream cones in additional mini-muffin cups.

2. Prepare cake mix batter according to package directions. Fill each greased muffin cup with 1 Tbsp. batter. Divide remaining batter among ice cream cones (scant 2 Tbsp. each).

3. Bake 15-20 minutes or until a toothpick inserted in center comes out clean. Cool in pans 5 minutes. Transfer both plain and cone cupcakes to wire racks; cool completely.

4. For frosting, beat butter and shortening until blended. Gradually beat in confectioners' sugar, milk and vanilla on medium speed until soft peaks form.

5. To assemble, spread a small amount of frosting on bottom of each plain cupcake; attach each to the top of a cone cupcake. Spread remaining frosting over tops of cupcakes, rounding each top to resemble a scoop of ice cream. Freeze until frosting is firm, 5-10 minutes.

6. For glaze, in a large metal bowl over simmering water, melt chocolate and shortening, stirring until smooth. Dip tops of cones in chocolate mixture. Decorate with sprinkles. Let stand until set.

1 CONE 445 cal., 23g fat (10g sat. fat), 44mg chol., 224mg sod., 61g carb. (48g sugars, 2g fiber), 2g pro.

Have Some Fun

Decorate the cones with different family members' favorite colors or to match a special occasion. School colors are festive too!

SKILL LEVEL 3

Two-Berry Pavlova

I first tried this dessert in Ireland. I made it for my kids at home, who loved to build their own with whipped cream and their favorite fruits.
—Norma Stevenson, Eagan, MN

PREP: 20 min. + standing • **BAKE:** 45 min. + cooling • **MAKES:** 12 servings

INGREDIENTS

- 4 **large egg whites, room temperature**
- ½ **tsp. cream of tartar**
- 1 **cup sugar**
- 1 **Tbsp. cornstarch**
- 1 **tsp. lemon juice**

TOPPINGS

- 2 **cups fresh blackberries**
- 2 **cups sliced fresh strawberries**
- ¼ **cup plus 3 Tbsp. sugar, divided**
- 1¼ **cups heavy whipping cream**

EQUIPMENT

- **Bowls**
- **Baking sheet**
- **Ruler**
- **Measuring cups & spoons**
- **Mixer**
- **Kitchen spoon**
- **Knife & cutting board**

1. Place egg whites in a large bowl. Line a baking sheet with parchment; draw a 10-in. circle on paper. Invert paper. Preheat oven to 300°. Add cream of tartar to egg whites; beat on medium speed until soft peaks form. Gradually add sugar, 1 Tbsp. at a time, beating on high after each addition. Continue beating until stiff glossy peaks form. Fold in cornstarch and lemon juice.

2. Spoon meringue onto prepared pan; with the back of a spoon, shape into a 10-in. circle, forming a shallow well in the center. Bake until meringue is set and dry, 45-55 minutes. Turn off oven (do not open oven door); leave meringue in oven 1 hour. Remove from oven; cool completely on baking sheet.

3. Toss berries with ¼ cup sugar; let stand 10 minutes. In a large bowl, beat cream until it begins to thicken. Add remaining sugar; beat until soft peaks form. Remove meringue from parchment; place on a serving plate. Spoon whipped cream over top, forming a slight well in the center. Top with berries.

1 PIECE 208 cal., 9g fat (6g sat. fat), 34mg chol., 29mg sod., 30g carb. (27g sugars, 2g fiber), 2g pro. **DIABETIC EXCHANGES** 2 starch, 2 fat.

Decorated Classic

My son Ryan and his cousins who were visiting helped me make, and then they decorated, a pavlova for their grandma's birthday. It's fun for kids to create designs with the fruit.
—Elizabeth B., mom

Ryan B., age 13; Cooper B., age 8; Tristan B., age 8; and Braden B., age 12, topped their pavlova with lemon curd, "frosted" it with whipped cream, then decorated it.

SKILL LEVEL 1

Easy Banana Muffins

These muffins go over well with kids. Not only are the treats loaded with bananas, but they're ready—start to finish—in just half an hour!
—Lorna Greene, Harrington, ME

INGREDIENTS

1½ cups all-purpose flour

1 cup sugar

1 tsp. baking soda

½ tsp. salt

3 medium ripe bananas

1 large egg, room temperature

⅓ cup vegetable oil

1 tsp. vanilla extract

EQUIPMENT

- Bowls
- Measuring cups & spoons
- Potato masher or mixer
- Kitchen spoon
- Muffin tin
- Wire rack

PREP: 10 min. • **BAKE:** 20 min. +cooling • **MAKES:** 1 dozen

1. In a large bowl, combine the dry ingredients. In another bowl, mash the bananas. Add egg, oil and vanilla; mix well. Stir into the dry ingredients just until moistened. Fill greased or paper-lined muffin cups half full.

2. Bake at 375° for 18-22 minutes or until a toothpick inserted in the center comes out clean. Cool for 10 minutes; remove from pan to a wire rack to cool completely.

1 MUFFIN 209 cal., 7g fat (1g sat. fat), 18mg chol., 209mg sod., 36g carb. (22g sugars, 1g fiber), 2g pro.

How to Mash Bananas

Use a potato masher to quickly mash ripe bananas. Choose bananas that are yellow with lots of brown spots (the kind you'd normally think are too ripe to eat on their own). These are the best for baking!

Elias F., age 2, uses a scoop to make his banana muffins all the same size.

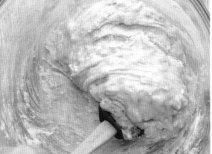

PAGE
232

HOLIDAY FAVES

SKILL LEVEL 2

Heart's Desire Pizza

Sweethearts of all ages will have fun sprinkling these personal pizzas with whatever toppings they love most.
—*Taste of Home* **Test Kitchen**

INGREDIENTS

- 1 tube (16.3 oz.) large refrigerated flaky biscuits
- 1 jar (14 oz.) pizza sauce

  Optional toppings: Sliced ripe olives, sliced and quartered pepperoni, chopped fresh mushrooms, chopped green and sweet yellow pepper
- 1½ cups shredded mozzarella cheese
- 1½ cups shredded cheddar cheese

EQUIPMENT

- Ruler
- Baking sheets
- Rolling pin
- Knife
- Spoon

PREP: 25 min. • **BAKE:** 10 min. • **MAKES:** 8 individual pizzas

1. Cut eight 6-in.-square pieces of aluminum foil; place on baking sheets. Lightly coat foil with cooking spray; set aside.

2. On a lightly floured surface, roll each biscuit to a 5-in. square. Cut a 1-in. triangle from the center top and place on the center bottom, reshaping the dough as needed to form a heart. Press edges to seal. Transfer to foil squares.

3. Spoon pizza sauce over dough to within ¼ in. of edges. If desired, sprinkle with toppings. Top with cheeses. Bake at 425° for 10-15 minutes or until golden brown.

1 PIZZA 342 cal., 19g fat (9g sat. fat), 38mg chol., 925mg sod., 30g carb. (7g sugars, 2g fiber), 13g pro.

Mini Frozen Pizzas

Little pizzas made on English muffins or bagels are the perfect after-school snack. Make a bunch (mini bagels work too), then freeze them on a cookie sheet until firm. Store in a freezer container with waxed paper between layers. When you're ready to eat, just bake or microwave until hot, let them cool a bit, and enjoy. You can even make different flavors to keep things fun!

"I make pizza dough and my kids pick sauces, veggies, meats and cheeses to put on top. Our rule is, they have to choose at least one veggie for their pizza. My brother sets up a sandwich bar the same way with his kids."

–KIRSTEN O., MOM

"I do a lot of measuring and weighing ingredients, and I like adding stuff to the stand mixer. Taste testing is the best part, though."

—ROWAN C., AGE 9

SKILL LEVEL 3

Cherry Meringue Dessert

Who can resist luscious cherries floating over a rich, creamy layer tucked inside a crispy shell? This tempting dessert looks almost too good to eat, but don't let that stop you—it's sure to impress your sweetheart.

—Kay Curtis, Guthrie, OK

PREP: 20 min. • **BAKE:** 1½ hours + cooling • **MAKES:** 6 servings

INGREDIENTS

3 large egg whites

¼ tsp. cream of tartar

¾ cup sugar

FILLING

3 oz. cream cheese, softened

¼ cup confectioners' sugar

½ tsp. vanilla extract

1 cup heavy whipping cream, whipped

1 can (21 oz.) cherry pie filling

EQUIPMENT

- Bowls
- Measuring cups & spoons
- Mixer
- Baking sheet
- Kitchen spoon
- Spatula

1. Place egg whites in a small bowl; let stand at room temperature for 30 minutes. Add cream of tartar; beat on medium speed until soft peaks form. Gradually beat in sugar, 1 Tbsp. at a time, on high until stiff glossy peaks form and sugar is dissolved.

2. Spoon meringue onto a parchment-lined baking sheet. Using the back of a spoon, form meringue into a 9-in. heart shape, building up edges slightly.

3. Bake at 275° for 1½ hours. Turn oven off and do not open door; leave meringue in oven for 1 hour. Remove from the oven; cool completely.

4. In a small bowl, beat the cream cheese, confectioners' sugar and vanilla until smooth. Using a spatula, fold in whipped cream. To serve, place heart on a serving platter; fill with cream cheese mixture and top with pie filling.

1 PIECE 413 cal., 19g fat (12g sat. fat), 60mg chol., 102mg sod., 57g carb. (52g sugars, 1g fiber), 4g pro.

How to Test Your Meringue

Stiff peaks are achieved when the whites stand up in points, rather than curling over. If you tilt the bowl, the whites shouldn't move. Sugar is dissolved when the mixture feels silky smooth between your fingers.

SKILL LEVEL 2

Be-Mine Sandwich Cookies

These simple cookies are the first thing to disappear from dessert tables. They're cute, colorful and extremely fast to make.

—Darcie Cross, Novi, MI

INGREDIENTS

- **6** oz. white or milk chocolate candy coating, coarsely chopped
- **50** Oreo cookies
  Assorted candy sprinkles or decorations

EQUIPMENT

- Knife & cutting board
- Bowl
- Microwave
- Spoon
- Offset spatula

TAKES: 20 min. • **MAKES:** 50 cookies

In a microwave, melt 2 oz. of candy coating at a time, stirring until smooth. Spread over cookie tops; decorate immediately. Place on waxed paper until set.

1 COOKIE 65 cal., 3g fat (1g sat. fat), 0 chol., 67mg sod., 9g carb. (6g sugars, 0 fiber), 1g pro.

★ ★ ★ ★ ★

"A treat that kids can easily put together. As an added bonus, nothing goes wrong with Oreos! Depending on the color of sprinkles that one uses, these are perfect for any occasion, including fall and Christmas. Something kids can give to teachers and friends."

—FROMBRAZILTOYOU, TASTEOFHOME.COM

Lucky Irish Punch

Beat 1 qt. softened **lime sherbet**, ½ cup thawed **limeade concentrate** and 2 Tbsp. **sugar**. Stir in 2 cans (12 oz. each) chilled **lemon-lime soda** and 1-2 cups **crushed ice**.

SKILL LEVEL **2**

INGREDIENTS

- ½ cup Cocoa Krispies, coarsely crushed
- 3 small scoops chocolate ice cream
- ½ cup plus 1 tsp. seedless strawberry jam, divided
- ¼ tsp. hot fudge ice cream topping
- 1 loaf (10¾ oz.) frozen pound cake, thawed
- ⅓ cup marshmallow creme
- 2 tsp. sweetened shredded coconut, toasted
- 1 Tbsp. unsalted sunflower kernels

EQUIPMENT

- Bowls
- Measuring cups & spoons
- Ice cream scoop
- Microwave
- Kitchen spoon
- Knife & cutting board
- Pastry brush

April Fool's Meatball Sub

Do you have a fun-loving family that appreciates food pranks? Give 'em a gotcha they'll never forget. This sub features a bun made from pound cake, and the meatballs are really ice cream. It's as fun to make as it is to eat.
—*Taste of Home* Test Kitchen

PREP: 20 min. + freezing • **MAKES:** 6 servings

1. Place cereal in a shallow bowl. Roll ice cream scoops in cereal to coat. Cover and freeze for 1 hour or until firm.

2. In a small microwave-safe bowl, combine ½ cup jam and ice cream topping. Microwave on high for 10-20 seconds or until warmed. Cut pound cake in half horizontally. Place bottom half on a serving plate. Spoon half of the jam mixture over cake; top with ice cream scoops, remaining jam mixture, marshmallow creme and coconut. Replace cake top.

3. In another microwave-safe bowl, melt remaining jam. Brush over top of cake; sprinkle with the sunflower kernels. Serve immediately.

1 SERVING 347 cal., 14g fat (7g sat. fat), 79mg chol., 177mg sod., 53g carb. (39g sugars, 1g fiber), 4g pro.

Sunny-Side-Up Dessert

Spread 1 tsp. **softened butter** on 1 slice of **pound cake**. Toast pound cake in a small skillet on both sides. Top with 2-3 Tbsp. **vanilla yogurt** and a **canned apricot half**.

SKILL LEVEL 2

INGREDIENTS

- 6 oz. white candy coating, coarsely chopped
- 6 drops green food coloring
- 1 drop yellow food coloring
- 1 cup sweetened shredded coconut
- 36 jelly beans

EQUIPMENT

- Knife & cutting board
- Bowl
- Microwave
- Kitchen spoon
- Measuring spoon

Coconut Egg Nests

Looking for an Easter activity that kids will enjoy assembling and eating? Try these sweet birds' nest cookies. They're a snap to make and call for just a few ingredients.

—Tonya Hamrick, Wallace, WV

TAKES: 20 min. • **MAKES:** 1 dozen

In a microwave, melt candy coating; stir in food coloring until blended. Stir in coconut. Drop by tablespoonfuls onto waxed paper into 12 mounds. Make an indentation in the center of each with the end of a wooden spoon handle. Fill each with 3 jelly beans. Let stand until set.

1 SERVING 127 cal., 7g fat (6g sat. fat), 0 chol., 22mg sod., 17g carb. (15g sugars, 0 fiber), 0 pro.

Jelly Bean Bark

Coarsely chop and melt 1¼ lbs. **white candy coating**; melt in a microwave, stirring occasionally. Line a 15x10x1-in. pan with foil; grease foil with 1 Tbsp. **butter**. Spread candy coating into prepared pan. Top with 2 cups **small jelly beans**, pressing to adhere. Let stand until set. Break bark into pieces.

How to Pack Peep Nests for Gifting

Place jelly beans and candy eggs in small food bags, then top each with a Peep Nest. Gently secure bag with a ribbon or twist tie. For a little sparkle, include pastel foil-wrapped kisses or other candies.

INGREDIENTS

- 2 pkg. (10 to 12 oz. each) white baking chips
- 1 pkg. (10 oz.) pretzel sticks
- 24 yellow chicks Peeps candy
- 1 pkg. (12 oz.) M&M's eggs or other egg-shaped candy

EQUIPMENT

- Large metal bowl and pan for melting baking chips
- Kitchen spoon
- Small bowl
- 2 forks

Peep Nests

I found one more thing to love about Peeps, the perennial springtime favorite: They make perfect mother birds for these pretzel nests with candy eggs.

—Jessica Boivin, Nekoosa, WI

PREP: 40 min. • **MAKES:** 2 dozen

1. In a large metal bowl over simmering water, melt baking chips; stir until smooth. Place about ½ cup melted chips in a small bowl for decorations; keep warm.

2. Add pretzel sticks to remaining chips; stir to coat evenly. Drop mixture into 24 mounds on waxed paper; shape into bird nests using 2 forks.

3. Dip bottoms of Peeps in reserved melted chips; place in nests. Attach eggs with remaining melted chips. Let stand until set.

1 NEST 276 cal., 11g fat (7g sat. fat), 7mg chol., 215mg sod., 41g carb. (30g sugars, 1g fiber), 4g pro.

"A new Easter tradition in our house! I may break the pretzel sticks in half next time to make smaller nests. Our three kids loved decorating them almost as much as eating them!"

—AHOLBERSMA, TASTEOFHOME.COM

INGREDIENTS

- 1 **scoop each vanilla, chocolate and strawberry ice cream**
- 1 **medium banana, peeled and split lengthwise**
- 2 **Tbsp. sliced fresh strawberries or 1 Tbsp. strawberry ice cream topping**
- 2 **Tbsp. pineapple chunks or 1 Tbsp. pineapple ice cream topping**
- 2 **Tbsp. whipped cream**
- 1 **Tbsp. chopped peanuts**
- 1 **Tbsp. chocolate syrup**
- 1 **Tbsp. caramel sundae syrup**
- 2 **maraschino cherries with stems**

EQUIPMENT

- Ice cream scoop
- Knife & cutting board
- Measuring spoon

All-American Banana Split

In 1904, the first banana split recipe was made here in Latrobe, Pennsylvania, by David Strickler, an apprentice pharmacist at a local drugstore. We still use his original formula when we make banana splits in our restaurants.

—**Melissa Blystone, Latrobe, PA**

TAKES: 5 min. • **MAKES:** 1 serving

Place ice cream in a dessert dish; add banana. Top with remaining ingredients. Serve immediately.

1 SERVING 710 cal., 31g fat (17g sat. fat), 88mg chol., 184mg sod., 107g carb. (68g sugars, 6g fiber), 11g pro.

Looking Good.

Want to make banana splits for the whole gang? Here's a trick for finishing a bunch of these all at once: Scoop the ice cream ahead of time! Place the scoops in their dishes or on a sheet pan, then freeze. Chop the strawberries and pineapple in advance, but split the bananas right before serving so they stay fresh.

Come dessert time, just grab your prepped ingredients and build those banana splits fast.

SKILL LEVEL 3

INGREDIENTS

- **1 package (10 oz.) miniature marshmallows**
- **3 Tbsp. canola oil**
- **1 tsp. watermelon extract, optional**
- **6 cups Rice Krispies**
- **¼ tsp. green paste food coloring**
- **¼ tsp. pink paste food coloring**
- **⅛ tsp. red paste food coloring**
- **⅓ cup miniature semisweet chocolate chips**

EQUIPMENT

- **Two saucepans**
- **Measuring cups & spoons**
- **Kitchen spoons**
- **Two 9-in. round cake pans**

Watermelon Rice Krispies Treats

Not only do these watermelon Rice Krispies treats look like your favorite summery fruit, they taste like 'em too!

—*Taste of Home* **Test Kitchen**

PREP: 30 min. + standing • **MAKES:** 2 dozen

1. In a large saucepan over low heat, melt marshmallows, oil and, if using, extract; stir until smooth. Remove from heat; remove half the mixture to another saucepan over low heat.

2. Stir in the green coloring; add 3 cups cereal and stir to combine. Stir the pink coloring and red coloring to remaining marshmallow mixture; add remaining 3 cups cereal and stir to combine.

3. Press half of green mixture around inside edge of a lightly greased 9-in. round cake pan, using waxed paper or a lightly greased spatula. Pack the center with half of pink mixture; press half of the chocolate chips into the surface of the pink portion. In a second cake pan, repeat with remaining mixtures and chips. Cool to room temperature. Cut each portion into 12 wedges.

1 PIECE 92 cal., 3g fat (1g sat. fat), 0 chol., 48mg sod., 17g carb. (9g sugars, 0 fiber), 1g pro.

Make It Your Own!

Instead of using 2 round cake pans, you can pack the green mixture into a greased metal bowl. Then add the pink and allow to set. Unmold your "half watermelon," cut it into wedges and press the mini chip seeds into each piece.

SKILL LEVEL **2**

ADULT HELP

BBQ Hot Dog & Potato Packs

INGREDIENTS

- 1 pkg. (20 oz.) refrigerated red potato wedges
- 4 hot dogs
- 1 small onion, cut into wedges
- ¼ cup shredded cheddar cheese
- ½ cup barbecue sauce

EQUIPMENT

- **Knife & cutting board**
- **Measuring cups**
- **Grill**
- **Tongs or turner**

Kids will have fun assembling these nifty foil packs, then savoring the tasty results in short order. They're great for camping.
—Kelly Westphal, Wind Lake, WI

TAKES: 20 min. • **MAKES:** 4 servings

1. Divide potato wedges among 4 pieces of heavy-duty foil (about 18 in. square). Top each with a hot dog, onion wedges and cheese. Drizzle with barbecue sauce. Fold foil around mixture, sealing tightly.

2. Grill, covered, over medium heat 10-15 minutes or until heated through. Open foil carefully to allow steam to escape.

1 SERVING 293 cal., 16g fat (7g sat. fat), 33mg chol., 1227mg sod., 25g carb. (9g sugars, 4g fiber), 11g pro.

★★★★★

"These little packs are delicious and so much fun to make! My family enjoyed customizing their packs by adding ingredients of their choice, including bell pepper strips. We will definitely make this recipe again!"
—GLAD2BMOM, TASTEOFHOME.COM

"You know the pudgy pie is ready when it's burnt a little bit."

—SOPHIA K., AGE 5

Milky Way Pudgy Pie

Butter 2 slices of **bread**. Make a sandwich in the pie iron, buttered side out, with a filling of 2 Tbsp. **miniature marshmallows**, 1 Tbsp. **graham cracker crumbs** and 1 **fun-size Milky Way candy bar**, chopped. Cook as directed.

ADULT HELP

Ham & Jack Pudgy Pie

Pepper jack cheese spices up these warm, melty sandwiches.
—Terri McKitrick, Delafield, WI

TAKES: 10 min. • **MAKES:** 1 serving

1. Place 1 slice bread in a greased sandwich iron. Top with ham, mushrooms, cheese, salsa and remaining bread slice. Close iron.

2. Cook over a hot campfire until golden brown and cheese is melted, 3-6 minutes, turning occasionally.

1 SANDWICH 268 cal., 9g fat (4g sat. fat), 33mg chol., 823mg sod., 32g carb. (4g sugars, 2g fiber), 15g pro. **DIABETIC EXCHANGES** 2 starch, 2 medium-fat meat

INGREDIENTS

- 2 slices sourdough bread
- 2 Tbsp. diced fully cooked ham
- 2 Tbsp. canned sliced mushrooms
- 3 Tbsp. shredded pepper jack cheese
- 1 Tbsp. salsa

EQUIPMENT

- Pudgy pie iron
- Knife & cutting board
- Measuring spoon
- Campfire or grill

Sophia K.'s favorite pie, banana, is ready to go on the fire.

Creative Campfire Cooking

Making pudgy pies around the campfire is a great way to spend family time outdoors! Sophia K.'s mom, Andrea, kicks off breakfast with crescent rolls, sausage, cheese and egg. Her dad, Steven, piles on pizza toppings like cheese, pepperoni, sausage, onions and peppers. Sophia's sister, Ellie, age 7, makes dessert with raspberries, chocolate, cream cheese and gooey marshmallow. Sophia loves peanut butter, banana, chocolate and marshmallow all squished together—so sweet! Everyone toasts their pies until crispy, then shares bites of their tasty creations.

SKILL LEVEL **1**

ADULT HELP

Sugar Cookie S'mores

Change up traditional s'mores by using sugar cookies and candy bars in place of the traditional ingredients. This fun twist on the campfire classic will delight everyone!
—*Taste of Home* **Test Kitchen**

TAKES: 15 min. • **MAKES:** 4 servings

INGREDIENTS

- 8 **fun-size Milky Way candy bars**
- 8 **sugar cookies (3 in.)**
- 4 **large marshmallows**

EQUIPMENT

- **Grill or campfire**
- **Grill rack**
- **Long-handled fork**

1. Place 2 candy bars on each of 4 cookies; place on grill rack. Grill, uncovered, over medium-high heat for 1-1½ minutes or until bottoms of cookies are browned.

2. Meanwhile, using a long-handled fork, toast marshmallows 6 in. from the heat until golden brown, turning occasionally. Remove marshmallows from fork and place over candy bars; top with remaining cookies. Serve immediately.

1 SANDWICH COOKIE 271 cal., 10g fat (5g sat. fat), 13mg chol., 123mg sod., 43g carb. (31g sugars, 1g fiber), 3g pro.

How to Make a S'mores Board

START WITH A BASE. Graham crackers are great, but try chocolate chip cookies or Oreos for a twist!

ADD A SPREAD. Spread Nutella, frosting or peanut butter on your base for extra yum.

CHOOSE A CHOCOLATE. Milk chocolate is classic, but try white chocolate or peanut butter cups for fun flavors.

BE PLAYFUL! Add crunch with pretzels or a kiss of fruit with sliced strawberries or bananas.

MIX UP THE 'MALLOWS. Plain marshmallows rock, but try chocolate or caramel ones to take your s'more to the next level.

"Choose any flavor candy you want, but it has to have chocolate and a marshmallow."
—ELLIE K., AGE 7

Ellie K.'s signature Girl Scout cookie s'more includes 1 Thin Mint, 1 Caramel deLite, strawberry marshmallow, a peanut butter cup and fudge frosting!

SKILL LEVEL 2

ADULT HELP

Peanut Butter Popcorn Balls

INGREDIENTS

- 5 **cups popped popcorn**
- 1 **cup dry roasted peanuts**
- ½ **cup sugar**
- ½ **cup light corn syrup**
- ½ **cup chunky peanut butter**
- ½ **tsp. vanilla extract**
- 10 **lollipop sticks**

EQUIPMENT

- **Large bowl**
- **Measuring cups & spoon**
- **Large heavy saucepan**
- **Kitchen spoon**
- **Ruler**

Friends and family are always happy to see these popcorn balls. I love making them just as much as eating them!
—Betty Claycomb, Alverton, PA

PREP: 20 min. + standing • **MAKES:** 10 servings

1. Place popcorn and peanuts in a large bowl. In a large heavy saucepan over medium heat, bring sugar and corn syrup to a rolling boil, stirring occasionally. Remove from the heat; stir in peanut butter and vanilla. Quickly pour over popcorn mixture and mix well.

2. When cool enough to handle, quickly shape into ten 2½-in. balls; insert a lollipop stick into each ball. Let stand at room temperature until firm; wrap in plastic.

1 POPCORN BALL 281 cal., 16g fat (2g sat. fat), 0 chol., 228mg sod., 32g carb. (25g sugars, 3g fiber), 7g pro.

Candy Corn Pudding Pops

Whisk a 3.4-oz. package of **instant cheesecake pudding mix** with 2 cups **2% milk** and ½ cup **heavy cream**. With **food coloring**, make one-third orange and one-third yellow. Add in layers to 8 freezer pop molds.

INGREDIENTS

¾ cup butter, melted

1½ cups sugar

1½ tsp. vanilla extract

3 large eggs, room temperature

¾ cup all-purpose flour

½ cup baking cocoa

½ tsp. baking powder

¼ tsp. salt

1 can (16 oz.) vanilla frosting

Orange paste food coloring

Green and black decorating gels

Optional: Candy corn and milk chocolate M&M's

EQUIPMENT

• Bowls

• Measuring cups & spoons

• Kitchen spoon

• Whisk

• 13x9-in. baking pan

• Wire rack

• Knife

• 3-in. pumpkin cookie cutter

• Small offset spatula or butter knife

Jack-o'-Lantern Brownies

Hosting a Halloween party? Use a cookie cutter to easily cut these homemade chocolate brownies into pumpkin shapes, then give them personality with orange, black and green frosting. Our grandchildren think these are the best.

—Flo Burtnett, Gage, OK

PREP: 20 min. • **BAKE:** 20 min. + cooling • **MAKES:** about 1 dozen

1. In a large bowl, beat butter, sugar and vanilla until well blended. Beat in eggs. Whisk the flour, cocoa, baking powder and salt; gradually add to butter mixture and mix well.

2. Line a greased 13x9-in. baking pan with waxed paper; grease the paper. Spread the batter evenly in pan. Bake at 350° until brownies begin to pull away from sides of pan, 18-22 minutes. Cool on a wire rack.

3. Run a knife around edge of pan. Invert brownies onto a work surface and remove waxed paper. Cut brownies with a 3-in. pumpkin cookie cutter, leaving at least ⅛ in. between each shape. (Discard scraps or save for another use.)

4. Tint frosting with orange food coloring; frost brownies. Use green gel to create the pumpkin stems and black gel and candy corn and M&M's to decorate the faces if desired.

1 BROWNIE 418 cal., 19g fat (11g sat. fat), 77mg chol., 259mg sod., 60g carb. (47g sugars, 1g fiber), 3g pro.

> **"Everybody loves brownies, and I love baking them."**
> **–AIDEN S., AGE 14**

SKILL LEVEL 1

Reese's Chocolate Snack Cake

This cake is constantly requested by my family. Its yellow and orange toppings make it the perfect dessert for a Halloween party.

—Eileen Travis, Ukiah, CA

PREP: 15 min. • **BAKE:** 30 min. + cooling • **MAKES:** 20 servings

INGREDIENTS

3⅓ cups all-purpose flour

⅔ cup sugar

⅔ cup packed brown sugar

½ cup baking cocoa

2 tsp. baking soda

1 tsp. salt

2 cups water

⅓ cup canola oil

⅓ cup unsweetened applesauce

2 tsp. white vinegar

1 tsp. vanilla extract

1 cup Reese's Pieces

½ cup coarsely chopped salted peanuts

EQUIPMENT

• 13x9-in. baking pan

• Bowls

• Measuring cups & spoons

• Whisk

• Kitchen spoon

• Wire rack

1. Preheat oven to 350°. Coat a 13x9-in. pan with cooking spray.

2. Whisk together first 6 ingredients. In another bowl, whisk together water, oil, applesauce, vinegar and vanilla. Add to flour mixture, stirring just until blended. Transfer to prepared pan. Sprinkle with Reese's Pieces and peanuts.

3. Bake 30-35 minutes or until a toothpick inserted in the center comes out clean. Cool on a wire rack.

1 PIECE 240 cal., 8g fat (2g sat. fat), 0 chol., 280mg sod., 38g carb. (19g sugars, 2g fiber), 5g pro.

Ghost Cream Cones

Mix **cake mix** of your choice. Stand 30 **ice cream cones** in muffin tins; add scant 3 Tbsp. cake batter to each. Bake at 350° for 17 minutes . Cool; pipe on **whipped topping** to make ghosts. Add facial features with **black decorating gel**.

Myla P., age 4, makes Rice Krispies treats with her grandma, Jill P. For special occasions, Myla's family decorates their treats with colored sprinkles.

SKILL LEVEL
3

INGREDIENTS

¼ cup butter, cubed

4 cups miniature marshmallows

6 cups Rice Krispies

28 Oreo cookies

1½ cups chocolate frosting

1 pkg. (11 oz.) candy corn

28 malted milk balls

White candy coating

EQUIPMENT

- Large saucepan
- Measuring cups
- Kitchen spoon
- Ruler
- Small offset spatula
- Knife & cutting board
- Piping bag & small round pastry tip

Gobbler Goodies

The kids and I had a ball making these tasty turkeys for Thanksgiving one year. The treats would make a fun favor at each place setting on your Thanksgiving table—if your family doesn't gobble them up first!

—Sue Gronholz, Beaver Dam, WI

PREP: 30 min. • **COOK:** 5 min. + cooling • **MAKES:** 28 servings

1. In a large saucepan, melt butter. Add marshmallows; stir over low heat until melted. Stir in cereal. Cool for 10 minutes. With buttered hands, form cereal mixture into 1½-in. balls. Twist apart cookies. If desired, remove the filling with a small offset spatula and save for another use. Spread chocolate frosting over each cookie half.

2. Place 28 cookie halves under cereal balls to form a base for each turkey. Place 5 pieces of candy corn in a fan pattern on each remaining cookie half; press each half onto a cereal ball to form the tail. Attach 2 pieces of candy corn to each cereal ball to form wings.

3. Attach a malted milk ball head with frosting. Cut white tips off the additional candy corn for beaks; attach to heads with frosting. Place the melted white candy coating in a piping bag fitted with a small round tip; pipe onto head to form eyes. Let stand until set. Store, tightly covered, at room temperature.

1 TURKEY 222 cal., 6g fat (2g sat. fat), 0 chol., 125mg sod., 43g carb. (31g sugars, 1g fiber), 1g pro.

Make It Your Own!

These candy turkeys are a fun project for the whole family to gather around and make. You can use different colors of candy corn and frosting. If they're available, Oreo cookies with a chocolate filling (instead of white) might be easier to work with.

SKILL LEVEL 2

Beef & Spinach Lasagna

INGREDIENTS

- 1 lb. lean ground beef (90% lean)
- 1 medium onion, chopped
- 2 jars (24 oz. each) spaghetti sauce
- 4 garlic cloves, minced
- 1 tsp. dried basil
- 1 tsp. dried oregano
- 1 pkg. (10 oz.) frozen chopped spinach, thawed and squeezed dry
- 2 cups ricotta cheese
- 2 cups shredded part-skim mozzarella cheese, divided
- 9 no-cook lasagna noodles
- Minced fresh basil, optional

EQUIPMENT

- Large skillet with lid
- Kitchen spoon
- Knife & cutting board
- Strainer for cooked beef
- Measuring cups & spoons
- Large bowl
- 13x9-in. baking dish

Using no-cook noodles gives you a jump start on assembling this hearty main dish. It cuts nicely after standing for a few minutes, revealing flavorful layers.

—Carolyn Schmeling, Brookfield, WI

PREP: 40 min. • **BAKE:** 40 min. + standing • **MAKES:** 12 servings

1. Preheat oven to 375°. In a large skillet, cook beef and onion over medium heat until meat is no longer pink, crumbling beef; drain. Stir in spaghetti sauce, garlic, basil and oregano. Bring to a boil. Reduce heat; cover and simmer for 10 minutes. In a large bowl, mix together spinach, ricotta and 1 cup mozzarella cheese.

2. Spread 1½ cups meat sauce into a greased 13x9-in. baking dish. Top with 3 noodles. Spread 1½ cups sauce to edges of noodles. Top with half the spinach mixture. Repeat layers. Top with the remaining noodles, sauce and 1 cup mozzarella cheese.

3. Cover and bake for 30 minutes. Uncover; bake until bubbly, 10-15 minutes longer. Let stand for 10 minutes before cutting. If desired, top with minced fresh basil.

1 PIECE 281 cal., 11g fat (6g sat. fat), 50mg chol., 702mg sod., 26g carb. (11g sugars, 3g fiber), 20g pro.

> **"I enjoy cooking lasagna with my dad every Christmas Eve."**
> **—MADELEINE B., AGE 10**

SKILL LEVEL **1**

Pull-Apart Garlic Bread

People go wild over this golden, garlicky loaf whenever I serve it. There's intense flavor in every bite.

—Carol Shields, Summerville, PA

INGREDIENTS

- ¼ cup butter, melted
- 1 Tbsp. dried parsley flakes
- 1 tsp. garlic powder
- ¼ tsp. garlic salt
- 1 loaf (1 lb.) frozen white bread dough, thawed

EQUIPMENT

- Small bowl
- Measuring spoons
- Spoon
- Knife & cutting board
- Ruler
- 9x5-in. loaf pan

PREP: 10 min. + rising • **BAKE:** 30 min. • **MAKES:** 16 servings

1. In a small bowl, combine butter, parsley, garlic powder and garlic salt. Cut dough into 1-in. pieces; dip into butter mixture. Layer in a greased 9x5-in. loaf pan. Cover and let rise until doubled, about 1 hour.

2. Bake at 350° for 30 minutes or until golden brown.

1 SERVING 104 cal., 4g fat (2g sat. fat), 8mg chol., 215mg sod., 15g carb. (1g sugars, 1g fiber), 3g pro.

How to Peel a Head of Garlic

STEP 1: To quickly peel a head of garlic, use 2 stainless steel bowls. Use the base of 1 bowl to break up the head.

STEP 2: Place 1 bowl over the other and shake vigorously to remove the skins.

STEP 3: Presto! The peeled garlic is ready to use.

SKILL LEVEL 2

INGREDIENTS

20 **large marshmallows**

2 **Tbsp. butter**

Green food coloring

3 **cups cornflakes**

Red M&M's minis (about 2 Tbsp.)

EQUIPMENT

- **Bowl**
- **Microwave**
- **Kitchen spoon**
- **Ruler**

Christmas Wreath Treats

Cornflakes take the place of traditional rice cereal in these sweet no-bake treats from our Test Kitchen. Dressed up with green food coloring and red candies, they're a pretty addition to cookie platters and dessert buffets.

—*Taste of Home* Test Kitchen

PREP: 20 min. + standing • **COOK:** 5 min. • **MAKES:** 8 servings

1. Place marshmallows and butter in a microwave-safe bowl; microwave, uncovered, on high until the butter is melted and marshmallows are puffed, about 45 seconds. Tint with green food coloring. Stir in cornflakes.

2. On a waxed paper-lined baking sheet, divide mixture into 8 portions. With buttered hands, working quickly, shape each portion into a 3-in. wreath. Decorate immediately with M&M's, pressing to adhere. Let stand until set.

1 WREATH 134 cal., 4g fat (2g sat. fat), 9mg chol., 116mg sod., 25g carb. (13g sugars, 0 fiber), 1g pro.

Looking Good.

Follow these pointers for picture-perfect Christmas wreaths.

BUTTER UP! Grease your hands and the waxed paper—this keeps the mixture from sticking and helps you move the wreaths easily. Cooking spray works for this too.

SHAPE YOUR WREATHS. First, press the cereal mixture into flat, tight circles so they don't fall apart. Then, gently poke a hole in the middle of each and widen it to make the wreath shape.

DECORATE. Consider an icing drizzle, shoestring licorice ribbons or Christmas light–shaped sprinkles.

SKILL LEVEL 2

INGREDIENTS

- 4 cups half-and-half cream
- 7 oz. white baking chocolate, chopped
- 2 oz. milk chocolate, chopped
- ¼ to ½ tsp. red food coloring
- ¼ to ½ tsp. peppermint extract
- Dash salt
- Optional: Sweetened whipped cream, candy canes and marshmallows

EQUIPMENT

- Large saucepan
- Measuring cup & spoon
- Knife & cutting board
- Whisk

Peppermint Red Velvet Drinking Chocolate

Add a festive touch to your next cup of drinking chocolate. The red velvet pairs nicely with the traditional peppermint and chocolate flavor combination.

—James Schend,
Pleasant Prairie, WI

TAKES: 20 min. • **MAKES:** 5 servings

In a large saucepan, heat cream over medium heat until bubbles form around side of pan (do not boil). Remove from heat; whisk in the chocolates, food coloring, extract and salt until smooth. Return to the heat; cook and stir until heated through. Pour into mugs; top with whipped cream, candy canes and marshmallows as desired.

1 CUP 512 cal., 34g fat (23g sat. fat), 100mg chol., 158mg sod., 39g carb. (38g sugars, 1g fiber), 10g pro.

How to Make Fancy Rims

Dip tops of mugs into melted candy coating, then into a bowl of sprinkles, finely chopped nuts or crushed peppermint candies. Another option is to decorate teaspoons the same way. Use the fancy spoons to stir marshmallows, crushed candy, whipped cream or spices into your cocoa.

SKILL LEVEL **2**

Candy Cane Snowballs

Every year I bake dozens of different kinds of Christmas cookies to give to family and friends. Leftover candy canes inspired this recipe. The sweet snowballs are dipped in a white candy coating, then into crushed peppermint candy.

—Debby Anderson, Stockbridge, GA

INGREDIENTS

- 2 cups butter, softened
- 1 cup confectioners' sugar
- 1 tsp. vanilla extract
- 3½ cups all-purpose flour
- 1 cup chopped pecans
- 8 oz. white candy coating, melted
- ⅓ to ½ cup crushed peppermint candies

EQUIPMENT

- Bowls
- Measuring cups & spoon
- Mixer or kitchen spoon
- Ruler
- Baking sheets
- Wire racks

PREP: 30 min. + chilling • **BAKE:** 15 min. + cooling • **MAKES:** about 5 dozen

1. Cream butter and confectioners' sugar until light and fluffy, 3-4 minutes. Beat in vanilla. Gradually beat in flour. Stir in pecans. Refrigerate, covered, until firm enough to shape, 3-4 hours.

2. Preheat oven to 350°. Shape dough into 1-in. balls. Place 2 in. apart on ungreased baking sheets.

3. Bake until lightly browned, about 15 minutes. Remove from pans to wire racks; cool completely.

4. Dip tops of cookies into candy coating, allowing excess to drip off; dip into crushed candies. Let stand until set.

1 COOKIE 123 cal., 9g fat (5g sat. fat), 16mg chol., 49mg sod., 11g carb. (5g sugars, 0 fiber), 1g pro.

How to Crush Candy Canes

To quickly (and neatly!) crush candy canes, place the candies in a heavy-duty resealable bag and crush them with a rolling pin.

SKILL LEVEL 3

INGREDIENTS

- 1 cup butter, softened
- 1½ cups confectioners' sugar
- 1 large egg
- 1 tsp. vanilla extract
- ½ tsp. almond extract
- 2½ cups all-purpose flour
- 1 tsp. baking soda
- 1 tsp. cream of tartar

FROSTING

- 3¾ cups confectioners' sugar
- 3 Tbsp. butter, softened
- 1 tsp. vanilla extract
- 2 to 4 Tbsp. 2% milk

  Optional: Food coloring and assorted sprinkles

EQUIPMENT

- Bowls
- Measuring cups & spoons
- Mixer or kitchen spoon
- Rolling pin
- Ruler
- Cookie cutters
- Baking sheets
- Wire racks
- Small offset spatula

Christmas Cutouts

Making and decorating these tender sugar cookies left a lasting impression on our four children. Now that they're grown, they've all asked for my recipe, baking memories with their own children.
—Shirley Kidd, New London, MN

PREP: 25 min. + chilling • **BAKE:** 10 min./batch + cooling
MAKES: about 3½ dozen

1. Cream butter and confectioners' sugar until light and fluffy, 3-4 minutes. Beat in egg and extracts. In another bowl, combine flour, baking soda and cream of tartar; gradually beat into the creamed mixture. Shape into a disk; securely wrap in waxed paper. Refrigerate until firm enough to roll, 2-3 hours.

2. Preheat oven to 375°. On a lightly floured surface, roll dough to ⅛-in. thickness. Cut with floured 2-in. cookie cutters. Place on ungreased baking sheets.

3. Bake until edges begin to brown, 7-8 minutes. Remove from pan to wire racks; cool completely.

4. For frosting, beat confectioners' sugar, butter, vanilla and enough milk to reach desired consistency; tint with food coloring if desired. Spread over cookies. Decorate as desired.

1 COOKIE 134 cal., 5g fat (3g sat. fat), 18mg chol., 74mg sod., 21g carb. (15g sugars, 0 fiber), 1g pro.

> **"Christmas cookies make my heart happy."**
> —STELLA R., AGE 7

How to Frost Cookies

If you are making different colors, place frostings in separate bowls and color each. Use a small spatula or butter knife to gently frost cookies. Add sprinkles and sugars before the frosting sets.

PAGE
252

BIRTHDAY CAKES
KIDS LOVE

(FUN IDEAS THAT GROWN-UPS CAN MAKE)

INGREDIENTS

- 4 large eggs, separated
- 4 oz. white baking chocolate, chopped
- ½ cup water
- 1 cup butter, softened
- 2 cups sugar
- 3 tsp. vanilla extract
- 2½ cups all-purpose flour
- 1 tsp. baking soda
- 1 cup buttermilk
- 1 cup sweetened shredded coconut
- 1 cup chopped pecans

FROSTING

- 2 pkg. (8 oz. each) cream cheese, softened
- 1 cup butter, softened
- 7½ cups confectioners' sugar
- 2 Tbsp. 2% milk
- 2 tsp. vanilla extract
- Brown food coloring

DECORATIONS

- Tootsie Roll Midgees
- 1 red Fruit Roll-Up

Puppy Dog Cake

A mouthwatering coconut cake was transformed into a pooch by adding chocolate, candy and a fruit snack to make a friendly face.
—Nancy Reichert, Thomasville, GA

PREP: 1 hour + standing • **BAKE:** 35 min. + cooling • **MAKES:** 16 servings

1. Let separated eggs stand at room temperature for 30 minutes.

2. In a microwave, heat white chocolate with water at 30% power until chocolate is melted; cool to room temperature.

3. In a large bowl, cream butter and sugar until light and fluffy, 5-7 minutes. Beat in the egg yolks, vanilla and white chocolate mixture. Combine flour and baking soda; add to creamed mixture alternately with buttermilk. In a small bowl, beat egg whites on high speed until stiff peaks form. Fold into white chocolate mixture with coconut and pecans.

4. Fill 4 greased muffin cups half full with batter. Spoon the remaining batter into 2 greased 9-in. round baking pans. Bake cupcakes at 350° for 15 minutes and cakes for 35 minutes or until a toothpick comes out clean. Cool for 10 minutes before removing from pans to wire racks to cool completely.

5. In a large bowl, beat cream cheese and butter. Add the confectioners' sugar, milk and vanilla. Color 1 cup of frosting brown; set aside.

6. Place 1 cake on a large platter or covered board (about 14x11 in.). Cut off cupcake tops; cut a ¼-in. piece from a rounded edge from each cupcake and discard. Place cut side of 2 cupcakes against side of cake with edges touching; frost top of cake and cupcakes with white frosting. Top with remaining cake and cupcakes; lightly frost top and sides.

7. Fill separate piping bags with the white and brown frostings. Using a grass piping tip, pipe 1 ear with white frosting on 1 ear with brown. Then, using a small star tip, pipe frosting on the top of the cake in white and brown.

8. Mold Tootsie Rolls into eyes, nose, brows and snout; place onto cake. With kitchen shears, cut Fruit Roll-Up into a 1-in. strip and round 1 end; place straight end under nose for the tongue. Add frosting accents if desired.

1 PIECE 841 cal., 44g fat (25g sat. fat), 137mg chol., 421mg sod., 109g carb. (91g sugars, 2g fiber), 7g pro.

★★★★★

"This is very cute and pretty easy to create. If you want to save time, just use a boxed cake mix or a more simple scratch cake recipe. This cake, made as directed, tasted really great and was moist too. The actual look of this cake was so cute! My 3-, 5-, and 7-year-olds loved it."

—HEATHERDTHOMAS, TASTEOFHOME.COM

EQUIPMENT

- Bowls
- Measuring cups & spoons
- Mixer or kitchen spoons
- Muffin tin
- Two 9-in. round baking pans
- Wire racks
- Knife & cutting board
- Offset spatula
- Piping bags
- Grass & star pastry tips
- Kitchen shears

INGREDIENTS

¼ cup butter, softened

¾ cup sugar

2 large eggs, room temperature

¾ tsp. vanilla extract

1 cup all-purpose flour

1 tsp. baking powder

½ tsp. salt

½ cup 2% milk

FROSTING

½ cup butter, softened

2½ cups confectioners' sugar

¼ tsp. vanilla extract

2 to 3 Tbsp. 2% milk

Sprinkles of your choice

EQUIPMENT

- Two 6-in. round baking pans
- Bowls
- Measuring cups & spoons
- Mixer or kitchen spoon
- Whisk
- Wire rack
- Offset spatula

Smash Cake

A smash cake is a small personalized cake given to a baby on their first birthday, allowing them to freely enjoy and smash the cake as part of a fun and messy photo opportunity.

—*Taste of Home* Test Kitchen

PREP: 30 min. • **BAKE:** 20 min. + cooling • **MAKES:** 6 servings

1. Preheat oven to 350°. Line bottoms of 2 greased and floured 6-in. round baking pans with parchment. In a small bowl, cream butter and sugar until crumbly. Add eggs, 1 at a time, beating well after each addition. Beat in vanilla. In another bowl, whisk flour, baking powder and salt; add to creamed mixture alternately with milk, beating well after each addition.

2. Transfer to prepared pans. Bake until a toothpick inserted in center comes out clean, 20-25 minutes. Cool in pans 10 minutes before removing to a wire rack; remove paper. Cool completely.

3. For frosting, in a small bowl, beat butter and confectioners' sugar until fluffy. Add vanilla and milk; beat until smooth. Spread frosting between layers and over top and sides of cake. Decorate as desired. Store in the refrigerator.

1 PIECE 610 cal., 25g fat (15g sat. fat), 125mg chol., 497mg sod., 92g carb. (76g sugars, 1g fiber), 5g pro.

A Smashing Photo-Shoot Success

Choose a simple background and ensure plenty of natural light to keep the photo's focus on your little one. Dress them comfortably in clothes that are easy to wash. Let your baby explore the cake and use video or take lots of snaps to capture those candid moments.

Yellow or white cake looks prettier in photos than chocolate cake.

INGREDIENTS

- 1 **pkg. white cake mix (regular size)**
- **Purple, blue, green, yellow, orange and red paste food coloring**
- 1 **cup heavy whipping cream**
- 3 **Tbsp. confectioners' sugar**
- ½ **tsp. vanilla extrac**
- **Sweetened whipped creamt**

EQUIPMENT

- **10-in. Bundt pan**
- **Bowls**
- **Measuring cups & spoons**
- **Mixer or kitchen spoon & whisk**
- **Six small bowls and spoons**
- **Seven small food-safe plastic bags**
- **Wire rack**

Rainbow Cake with Clouds

Some cakes stand on their own without icing. For this bright Rainbow Cake, use a little whipped cream to make fluffy clouds.

—Janet Tigchelaar, Ancaster, ON

PREP: 30 min. • **BAKE:** 40 min. + cooling • **MAKES:** 16 servings

1. Preheat oven to 325°. Grease and flour a 10-in. Bundt pan. Prepare cake mix according to package directions. Transfer 1⅓ cups batter to prepared pan; spread evenly. Remove an additional 2 Tbsp. batter to a small bowl; reserve.

2. Divide remaining batter into 6 separate bowls, tinting each with food coloring to make the following: 2 Tbsp. purple batter, ¼ cup blue batter, ⅓ cup green batter, ½ cup yellow batter, ⅔ cup orange batter, and the remaining batter red.

3. Fill 6 small food-safe plastic bags with color batters. Cut a small hole in a corner of the red bag; pipe a wide ring onto white batter to within ½ in. of pan edges. Pipe a ring of orange in the middle of the red ring, leaving some red visible on each side. Repeat with remaining colors, in rainbow color order. (Each ring will be narrower than the previous.) Fill a seventh bag with reserved white batter; pipe over purple ring only.

4. Bake 40-45 minutes or until a toothpick inserted in center comes out clean. Cool completely in pan on a wire rack.

5. Remove cake from pan; place on a serving plate. In a bowl, beat cream until it begins to thicken. Add confectioners' sugar and vanilla; beat until soft peaks form. Serve cake with whipped cream clouds.

NOTE To remove cake easily, use solid shortening to grease pan.

1 PIECE WITH 2 TBSP. WHIPPED CREAM 208 cal., 11g fat (4g sat. fat), 20mg chol., 216mg sod., 24g carb. (13g sugars, 0 fiber), 2g pro.

"Instructions are clear. Easy enough that my 10-year-old made it! Fun and easy recipe, especially for a rainy day or kids-themed party."

—PEANUTSNONA76, TASTEOFHOME.COM

How to Create the Rainbow

Use small bags and ever-decreasing quantities of batter to produce this rainbow design. Don't worry about being too perfect. When you slice into this cake, it'll be gorgeous!

INGREDIENTS

- ½ cup butter, softened
- 1½ cups sugar
- 2 large eggs, room temperature
- 1 tsp. vanilla extract
- 3 cups all-purpose flour
- ¾ tsp. salt
- ½ tsp. baking powder
- ½ tsp. baking soda
- 1 cup sour cream
- 1 can (16 oz.) vanilla frosting

  Optional toppings: Coarse sugar, sprinkles and additional frosting

EQUIPMENT

- Bowls
- Measuring cups & spoons
- Mixer or kitchen spoon
- Whisk
- 13x9-in. baking pan
- Wire rack
- Offset spatula
- Piping bags & pastry tips, optional

Sour Cream Sugar Cookie Cake

My husband requested a giant sugar cookie for his birthday. I wanted to do something a bit more exciting than that, so I came up with this sugar cookie cake. The secret to a dense yet cakelike texture is to not overbake it.

—Carmell Childs, Orangeville, UT

PREP: 20 min. + cooling • **BAKE:** 20 min. • **MAKES:** 20 servings

1. Preheat oven to 350°. In a large bowl, cream butter and sugar until light and fluffy, 5-7 minutes. Beat in the eggs and vanilla. In another bowl, whisk flour, salt, baking powder and baking soda; add to the creamed mixture alternately with sour cream, beating after each addition just until combined. Spread into a greased 13x9-in. baking pan.

2. Bake until a toothpick inserted in center comes out clean, 20-25 minutes. Cool completely on a wire rack. Spread frosting over top. Decorate with optional toppings as desired.

1 PIECE 295 cal., 11g fat (6g sat. fat), 34mg chol., 228mg sod., 46g carb. (29g sugars, 1g fiber), 3g pro.

Simple Sprinkles Variation

Instead of decorating the cake like a game jersey, take it easy and sprinkle your favorite sugars, sprinkles, candies or toppings over the top instead.

INGREDIENTS

- 2 pkg. chocolate cake mix (regular size)
- 1⅓ cups butter, softened
- 8 oz. unsweetened chocolate, melted and cooled
- 6 tsp. vanilla extract
- 7½ to 8 cups confectioners' sugar
- ⅓ to ½ cup milk
- Candy necklaces, foil-covered chocolate coins, candy rings or candies of your choice
- 2 pieces berry tie-dye Fruit Roll-Ups

EQUIPMENT

- Bowls
- Measuring cups & spoons
- Mixer or kitchen spoon
- Two 13x9-in. baking pans
- Wire racks
- Offset spatula
- 5 wooden skewers (three 4-in., two 7½-in.)
- Foil-covered heavy corrugated cardboard (12x7½ in.)
- Piping bag & star pastry tip
- Knife

Treasure Chest Cake

Swashbucklers of all ages were eager to seize a chocolaty piece of this birthday cake, although some guests thought it was too cute to cut! Folks were impressed with the edible treasure chest, and they loved the rich chocolate icing.

—Sharon Hanson, Franklin, TN

PREP: 45 min. • **BAKE:** 30 min. + cooling • **MAKES:** 24 servings

1. In 2 batches, prepare and bake cakes according to package directions, using 2 greased and floured 13x9-in. baking pans. Cool for 10 minutes; remove from pans to wire racks to cool.

2. In a large bowl, beat butter until fluffy; beat in the chocolate, vanilla, confectioners' sugar and enough milk to reach spreading consistency. Center 1 cake on a 16x12-in. covered board; frost top. Top with remaining cake; frost top and sides of cake. With an offset spatula, smooth frosting to resemble boards.

3. For chest lid, insert 4-in. skewers equally spaced into 1 long side of corrugated cardboard lid. Frost top of lid. Cut a small hole in the corner of a pastry or plastic bag; insert star tip. Pipe a shell border on edges of lid and for handles on side of chest.

4. Place one 7½-in. skewer on each side of cake top, about 3½ in. from back of chest. Position lid over cake; gently insert short skewers into cake about 1 in. from back of chest. Rest lid on long skewers.

5. Arrange candy on top of chest (under propped-up lid). Cut a small keyhole from a Fruit Roll-Up; center on front of cake. Position strips of Fruit Roll-Ups on front and back of chest.

1 PIECE 539 cal., 24g fat (11g sat. fat), 74mg chol., 424mg sod., 77g carb. (57g sugars, 3g fiber), 5g pro.

INGREDIENTS

- 2 pkg. white cake mix (regular size)
- 8 large eggs, room temperature
- 1 cup buttermilk
- 1 cup canola oil
- Blue, green, pink and yellow gel food coloring

FROSTING

- 8 cups confectioners' sugar
- 1½ cups butter, softened
- 2 tsp. vanilla extract
- 4 to 6 Tbsp. heavy whipping cream
- 1¼ cups assorted candy, sprinkles and mini white chips

EQUIPMENT

- Four 8-in. round baking pans
- Bowls
- Measuring cups & spoons
- Mixer or kitchen spoon
- Bread knife
- 3-in. round cutter
- Offset spatula
- Piping bags & pastry tips, optional

Surprise Cake

We filled our surprise cake with M&M's, sprinkles and mini chocolate chips, but there are other options. A few mini Oreos would be fun, as would Sixlets or malted milk balls. Get creative, but remember that you want the candies to easily to fall out of the cake. Sour Patch Kids and gummies might not come tumbling out of the cake on their own.
—Taste of Home Test Kitchen

PREP: 25 min. + decorating • **BAKE:** 30 min. + cooling • **MAKES:** 16 servings

1. Preheat oven to 350°. Line bottoms of 4 greased 8-in. round baking pans with parchment; grease paper. In a large bowl, combine cake mix, eggs, buttermilk and oil; mix until well combined, about 2 minutes. Divide batter among 4 bowls; tint 1 portion blue, second portion green, third portion pink and remaining portion yellow with food coloring. Transfer batters to prepared pans.

2. Bake until a toothpick inserted in the center comes out clean, 30-35 minutes. Cool in pans 10 minutes before removing to wire racks; remove paper. Cool completely. Using a bread knife, trim tops of cake layers to be level (save cake scraps for another use). For frosting, in a large bowl, beat confectioners' sugar, butter, vanilla and enough cream to reach desired consistency.

3. Using a 3-in. round cutter, cut a circle out of the center of the blue cake layer and the pink cake layer (save for another use). Place the green cake layer on a serving plate; spread with 1 cup frosting. Top with the pink layer and ¾ cup frosting. Repeat with blue layer and frosting. Fill center of cake with assorted candies and sprinkles. Top with the yellow cake layer.

4. Spread remaining frosting over top and side of cake. If desired, use additional frosting and sprinkles to decorate. Store in the refrigerator.

NOTE To substitute for each cup of buttermilk, use 1 Tbsp. white vinegar or lemon juice plus enough milk to measure 1 cup. Stir, then let stand 5 minutes. Or use 1 cup plain yogurt or 1¾ tsp. cream of tartar plus 1 cup milk.

1 PIECE 574 cal., 27g fat (13g sat. fat), 50mg chol., 353mg sod., 84g carb. (71g sugars, 0 fiber), 2g pro.

INGREDIENTS

1 cup butter, softened

2½ cups sugar

4 large eggs, room temperature

4 cups all-purpose flour

3 tsp. baking powder

1 tsp. salt

½ tsp. baking soda

1½ cups sour cream

FROSTING

6 oz. white baking chips

¼ cup heavy whipping cream

2 tsp. vanilla extract

6 large egg whites, room temperature

1½ cups sugar

½ tsp. cream of tartar

½ tsp. salt

2 cups unsalted butter, cubed

DECORATING

Blue, red and green liquid food coloring

4 oz. ready-to-use rolled fondant

Confectioners' sugar

2 candy eyes

Optional: Sea creature candies and graham cracker crumbs

Baby Shark Cake

It doesn't take much to add a fun theme to a birthday party. This creatively decorated cake will bring a Baby Shark *theme to life.*
—*Taste of Home* Test Kitchen

PREP: 1 hour • **BAKE:** 25 min. + cooling • **MAKES:** 16 servings

1. Preheat oven to 350°. Line bottoms of 3 greased and floured 9-in. round baking pans with parchment; grease paper. In a large bowl, cream butter and sugar until light and fluffy, 5-7 minutes. Add eggs, 1 at a time, beating well after each addition. Combine flour, baking powder, salt and baking soda; add to the creamed mixture alternately with sour cream, beating well after each addition.

2. Transfer to prepared pans. Bake until edges begin to brown, 25-30 minutes. Cool for 10 minutes before removing from pans to wire racks to cool completely.

3. In a microwave, melt baking chips with cream until smooth, stirring every 30 seconds. Stir in vanilla. Set aside to cool slightly. Meanwhile, in heatproof bowl of a stand mixer, whisk egg whites, sugar, cream of tartar and salt until blended. Place over simmering water in a large saucepan over medium heat. Whisking constantly, heat mixture until a thermometer reads 160°, 8-10 minutes.

4. Remove from heat. With whisk attachment of stand mixer, beat mixture on high speed until cooled to 90°, about 7 minutes. Gradually beat in butter, a few tablespoons at a time, on medium speed until smooth. Beat in cooled baking chip mixture until blended.

5. Set aside ¼ cup frosting. Tint remaining frosting desired shades of blue; spread blue frosting between layers and over top and side of cake. Tint ½ oz. fondant red. Divide remaining fondant in half. Tint 1 portion blue. Leave other half white. On a work surface dusted with confectioners' sugar, roll out blue fondant to ⅛-in. thickness. Using a 3-in. round cutter, cut out 1 circle; repeat with white fondant. Using a sharp knife, cut mouth opening, teeth and body shape on lower portion of white circle. Place white fondant cutout onto blue circle. Roll red fondant to ⅛-in. thickness; cut a small triangle and place in mouth opening, under white fondant and on top of blue fondant. If needed, brush fondant lightly with water to help layers adhere.

6. With remaining rolled blue fondant, cut a crescent moon shape for tail and a triangle for fin. Secure fin and tail to shark body, brushing edges lightly with water, if needed, to help pieces adhere. Secure candy eyes to shark body with small amount of reserved frosting. Cut in small slits for gills and nostrils. Place fondant shark on side of cake by pressing gently into frosting. Tint remaining reserved frosting green. Using a leaf tip, pipe seaweed on sides of cake. If desired, decorate cake with sea creature candies and graham cracker crumbs for sand. Refrigerate until serving.

1 PIECE 777 cal., 46g fat (28g sat. fat), 150mg chol., 503mg sod., 86g carb. (62g sugars, 1g fiber), 8g pro.

EQUIPMENT

- **Three 9-in. round baking pans**
- **Bowls**
- **Measuring cups & spoons**
- **Stand mixer with heatproof bowl**
- **Wire racks**
- **Microwave**
- **Offset spatula**
- **Rolling pin**
- **3-in. round cutter**
- **Knife**
- **Piping bag & leaf pastry tip**

INGREDIENTS

1 **cup butter, softened**

1¼ **cups sugar**

⅛ **tsp. pink paste food coloring**

3 **large eggs, room temperature**

1 **tsp. vanilla extract**

2½ **cups all-purpose flour**

1½ **tsp. baking powder**

¼ **tsp. baking soda**

¼ **tsp. salt**

1 **cup buttermilk**

WHITE CHOCOLATE GANACHE

2 **cups white baking chips**

½ **cup heavy whipping cream**

1 **Tbsp. butter**

Pink coarse sugar and sugar pearls

EQUIPMENT

- **Bowls**
- **Measuring cups & spoons**
- **Mixer or kitchen spoon**
- **Muffin tins**
- **Wire racks**
- **Small saucepan**
- **Whisk**
- **Offset spatula or piping bag & pastry tip**

Pink Velvet Cupcakes

My daughter loves all things pink, so this recipe was just right for her birthday. Even my teenage son (not a fan of pink) ate his share too.

—Paulette Smith,
  Winston-Salem, NC

PREP: 30 min. + chilling • **BAKE:** 25 min. + cooling • **MAKES:** 2 dozen

1. In a large bowl, cream the butter, sugar and food coloring until light and fluffy, 5-7 minutes. Add eggs, 1 at a time, beating well after each addition. Beat in vanilla. Combine the flour, baking powder, baking soda and salt; add to creamed mixture alternately with buttermilk, beating well after each addition.

2. Fill 24 paper-lined muffin cups two-thirds full. Bake at 350° until a toothpick inserted in the center comes out clean, 23-27 minutes. Cool for 10 minutes before removing from pans to wire racks to cool completely.

3. Meanwhile, place white chips in a small bowl. In a small saucepan, bring cream just to a boil. Pour over chips; whisk until smooth. Stir in butter. Transfer to a large bowl. Refrigerate for 30 minutes, stirring once. Beat on high speed until soft peaks form and frosting is light and fluffy, 2-3 minutes. Frost cupcakes. Top with coarse sugar and sugar pearls. Store in the refrigerator.

1 CUPCAKE 266 cal., 15g fat (9g sat. fat), 57mg chol., 154mg sod., 29g carb. (20g sugars, 0 fiber), 3g pro.

"Amazing. I made these for my daughter's fifth birthday because she wanted pink cupcakes for her princess tea party. For the frosting, I used chopped Baker's white chocolate instead of white chips because it melts better. It was hands-down the best frosting I have ever made. I will be making these cupcakes again!"

—LEEKY12, TASTEOFHOME.COM

INGREDIENTS

- 4 cups birthday cake-flavored ice cream or flavor of your choice, softened if necessary
- 1 funfetti cake mix (regular size)
- 1 carton (8 oz.) frozen whipped topping, thawed

  Sprinkles

EQUIPMENT

- Three 9-in. round baking pans
- Offset spatula
- Bowl
- Measuring cup
- Mixer or kitchen spoon
- Wire racks
- Bread knife
- Offset spatula

Funfetti Ice Cream Cake

When we were young, Mom made birthday cakes with a small toy on top, chosen just for us. Now that I'm a parent, I go with sprinkles.
—Becky Herges, Fargo, ND

PREP: 50 min. + freezing • **MAKES:** 12 servings

1. Line a 9-in. round pan with plastic wrap. Spread ice cream into pan. Freeze 2 hours or until firm.

2. Prepare and bake cake mix according to package directions, using two 9-in. round baking pans. Cool in pans 10 minutes before removing to wire racks to cool completely.

3. Using a bread knife, trim tops of cakes if domed. Place 1 cake layer on a serving plate. Invert ice cream onto cake layer; remove plastic wrap. Top with remaining cake layer. Spread whipped topping over top and side of cake. Decorate with sprinkles as desired. Freeze 2 hours longer or until firm.

1 PIECE 374 cal., 19g fat (8g sat. fat), 66mg chol., 315mg sod., 45g carb. (27g sugars, 1g fiber), 5g pro.

All-Star Ice Cream Cake

Mix **red and blue sprinkles** into **white cake mix** batter and **vanilla ice cream**. Top cake with star-shaped cutters, then gently spoon **nonpareils** into each. Add **edible glitter** to take it over the top!

EQUIPMENT

- Bowls
- Measuring cups & spoons
- Mixer or kitchen spoon
- Zesting tool
- Two 9-in. heart-shaped baking pans
- Offset spatula
- Wire racks
- Bread knife
- Piping bag & round pastry tip
- Channel knife

Looking Good.

This pretty butterfly stands out because of its use of complementary colors—opposites on the color wheel that pair well together, like blue and orange. Other complementary colors include purple and yellow, or red and green. Try experimenting with your own color combinations!

INGREDIENTS

1   cup butter, softened

2   cups sugar

3   large eggs

1   tsp. grated orange zest

1   tsp. orange extract

2   cups all-purpose flour

¼   tsp. salt

¼   tsp. baking soda

1   cup sour cream

FROSTING

¾   cup butter, softened

6   oz. cream cheese, softened

3   cups confectioners' sugar

1   tsp. vanilla extract

   Yellow gel or paste food coloring

   Colored sugars

   Gumdrops

   Orange peel

Butterfly Cake

Impress guests by making an adorable and delicious cake. It is actually easy to put together.

—Bonnie Jost, Manitowoc, WI

PREP: 1 hour + standing • **BAKE:** 25 min. + cooling • **MAKES:** 10 servings

1. Let eggs stand at room temperature for 30 minutes. In a large bowl, cream butter and sugar. Add the eggs, orange zest and extract; beat until combined. Combine the flour, salt and baking soda; add to the creamed mixture alternately with sour cream. Spoon into 2 greased 9-in. heart-shaped baking pans; spread evenly in pans. Bake at 350° for 25-30 minutes or until a toothpick inserted in the center comes out clean. Cool for 10 minutes before removing from pans to wire racks to cool completely.

2. Cut 1½ in. off the pointed ends of each heart cake; set aside. Place the large pieces on a 17x15-in. covered board, placing cut sides of hearts together, forming wings. Trim the reserved pointed end pieces to form the head and tail of the butterfly.

3. In a small bowl, cream the butter and cream cheese. Add the confectioners' sugar and vanilla. Remove ½ cup frosting and tint yellow; set aside. Frost cake sides and top with white frosting. Cut a small hole in the corner of a pastry or plastic bag; insert #6 round tip. Fill bag with remaining white frosting; set aside.

4. Frost a portion of each wing with yellow frosting. Decorate butterfly's body and wings with colored sugars. Pipe white frosting to separate colored sections on wings and to outline the body. Gently spread additional yellow frosting to build up the wing sections. Decorate the wings with gumdrops.

5. Using a channel knife, cut two 12-in.-long pieces of orange peel. Wrap around the handle of a wooden spoon. Remove from spoon and place above the body for antennae.

1 PIECE 775 cal., 40g fat (25g sat. fat), 174mg chol., 472mg sod., 99g carb. (76g sugars, 1g fiber), 6g pro.

INGREDIENTS

2¼ cups cake flour

1½ cups sugar

3½ tsp. baking powder

½ tsp. salt

½ cup unsalted butter, softened

4 large egg whites, room temperature

¾ cup 2% milk

2 tsp. vanilla extract

½ tsp. almond extract

BUTTERCREAM

½ cup butter

4 cups confectioners' sugar

1½ tsp. vanilla extract

5 to 6 Tbsp. 2% milk

Confetti sprinkles

Vanilla Birthday Cake

This simple, festive cake has been celebrated in my family for years. Dressed up with delicious buttercream and sprinkles, it becomes pure party fun.

—Sarah Tramonte, Milwaukee, WI

PREP: 30 min. • **BAKE:** 20 min. + cooling • **MAKES:** 16 servings

1. Preheat oven to 350°. Line bottoms of 2 greased 9-in. round baking pans with parchment; grease parchment.

2. In a large bowl, whisk flour, sugar, baking powder and salt. Beat in butter. Add the egg whites, 1 at a time, beating well after each addition. Gradually beat in milk and extracts.

3. Transfer batter to prepared pans. Bake 20-25 minutes or until a toothpick inserted in center comes out clean. Cool in pans 10 minutes before removing to wire racks; remove paper. Cool completely.

4. For buttercream, beat the butter in a large bowl until creamy. Beat in the confectioners' sugar, vanilla and enough milk to reach desired consistency. Frost and decorate cake as desired; finish with confetti sprinkles.

1 PIECE 435 cal., 24g fat (15g sat. fat), 62mg chol., 257mg sod., 51g carb. (35g sugars, 0 fiber), 4g pro.

How to Pipe Perfect Rosettes

Practice makes perfect, so fill your piping bag and twist the bag down to remove any air pockets. Then experiment with pressure and piping techniques on a piece of waxed paper or parchment before graduating to the cake. Scoop up and reuse the frosting as needed.

EQUIPMENT

- Two 9-in. round baking pans
- Bowls
- Measuring cups & spoons
- Whisk
- Mixer or kitchen spoon
- Wire racks
- Offset spatula
- Piping bag & pastry tip, optional

RECIPE INDEX